WHAT WOULD YOU DO IF YOU WERE MADE A GOD FOR A DAY?

WHAT WOULD YOU DO IF YOU WERE MADE A GOD FOR A DAY?

FRANKLIN D. TODD

Copyright © 2023 by Franklin Todd

All rights reserved. No part of this publication may be reproduced, distributed, or transmitted in any form or by any means, including photocopying, recording, or other electronic or mechanical methods, without the prior written permission of the copyright owner and the publisher, except in the case of brief quotations embodied in critical reviews and certain other noncommercial uses permitted by copyright law. For permission requests, write to the publisher, addressed "Attention: Permissions Coordinator," at the address below.

CITIOFBOOKS, INC.
3736 Eubank NE Suite A1
Albuquerque, NM 87111-3579
www.citiofbooks.com
Hotline: 1 (877) 389-2759
Fax: 1 (505) 930-7244

Ordering Information:
Quantity sales. Special discounts are available on quantity purchases by corporations, associations, and others. For details, contact the publisher at the address above.

Printed in the United States of America.

ISBN-13:	Softcover	978-1-960952-29-5
	Hardcover	978-1-960952-30-1
	eBook	978-1-960952-31-8

Library of Congress Control Number: 2023910194

Table of Contents

PREFACE : V

Chapter One : The Understanding of Being a God............................. 1

Chapter Two : Divine Encounter... 9

Chapter Three : The Blessings, The Pride, and The Temptation 14

Chapter Four : Walking the Heart of God... 20

Chapter Five : God Watches Even the Smallest Things 29

Chapter Six : Sorrowful World, Yet Wonderful World 34

Chapter Seven : The Walk of a New Man... 43

Chapter Eight : Who Is Your Neighbor?.. 49

Chapter Nine : The True Giver... 57

Chapter Ten : Tithing, The Church, and The Contradiction 68

GRATITUDE : 84

INTRODUCTION

"What Would You Do If You Were Made A God For A Day?" is a powerful and thought-provoking read that challenges readers to examine their beliefs and actions in light of the true essence of Christianity. Mr. Todd offers a compelling argument for the importance of love and selflessness in the practice of the Christian faith.

One of the key strengths of this book is its accessibility. Mr. Todd writes in a clear, straightforward style that is easy to understand, even for those who may not be well-versed in Christian theology. He presents his ideas in a conversational tone that invites readers to engage with his message and consider how it might apply to their own lives.

Throughout the book, Todd uses a series of hypothetical scenarios to illustrate his points. For example, he asks readers to imagine what they would do if they were given God-like powers for a day. Would they use those powers to benefit themselves, or would they use them to help others? This approach is effective in helping readers see the practical implications of the book's message and apply it to their own lives.

Another strength of the book is Mr. Todd's emphasis on the importance of love as the foundation of the Christian faith. He argues that love is not just an emotion or feeling, but an active choice that we must make every day. He challenges readers to examine their own lives and consider whether they are truly living in a selfless and loving way, or whether they are motivated by selfish desires.

While Mr. Todd's message is clear and compelling. At times, the writing can be repetitive, and some readers may find themselves wishing for more specific examples or practical advice on how to apply the book's message to their own lives.

Overall, however, "What Would You Do If You Were Made A God For A Day?" is a powerful and important book that has the potential to transform the way readers think about their faith and their relationship with others. Mr. Todd's emphasis on the importance of love and selflessness is a message that is sorely needed in our world today, and his book is a welcome addition to the literature on Christian spirituality.

1. "Love is stronger than our hearts and minds and shines brighter than our eyesight." by F.D.T.

2. "It is not what or how much we accumulate in life that reflects God's glory in us, but what is important to God is what we do with what we have accumulated in life." by F.D.T.

3. "It is the things we do as believers that reflect God's glory in us, and not that which we accumulate." by F.D.T.

4. "It is not the power that we possess that makes us gods to others, but what we do with the power that we possess." by F.D.T.

5. "True wealth is not measured by how much a man gathers, but how much he distributes." by F.D.T.

6. "Not every victory is joyful and not every disappointment is painful. Some victories bring weakness and sorrow, and some disappointments bring strength and wisdom." by F.D.T.

7. "It was one lie that crucified Jesus Christ, but it was one Truth that resurrected Him from the grave. Your one lie could set a whole city on fire, but your one truth could save a whole nation. Always endeavor to speak the truth in love and humility." by F.D.T.

8. "Man was born ordinary, but after his extraordinary accomplishments, he became great. Therefore, any ordinary man can be a great man, depending on the mercy, grace, and favor of God upon his life to make him accomplish great things." by F.D.T.

9. "There is good inside every man from which a person can benefit." by F.D.T.

10. "The foolishness of God is wiser than man, simply because God's foolishness is an expression of His mysterious power and wonder which can never be fully comprehended by

the natural mind. It sounded foolish when the young shepherd, David killed the veteran warrior, Goliath, with a single stone – That was God's foolishness which turned out to be man's mystery. It was also foolish for the young Saul to go in search of his father's asses and ended up being crowned a King. What may seem foolish to you could be God's mysterious power at work in your life. For example, Faith does not make any logic or sense to a realistic, logical and rational mind, simply because it is foolish to believe something you have not seen or physically arranged for. But it is that kind of foolishness that produces miraculous results beyond the human abilities and beyond belief." by F.D.T.

11. "The wicked would see many excuses in doing good things that wouldn't benefit him directly, but he would see or find no excuse in doing anything good or bad that would benefit him directly." by F.D.T.

12. "A nation's success or prosperity should not be measured by its infrastructural development; rather, it must be measured by the minimization of poverty, disease, ignorance, and illiteracy from amongst its citizens." by F.D.T.

PREFACE

Today, it is unfortunate to recognize how the Church of our Lord Jesus Christ has been overshadowed and controlled by the spirits of greed, selfishness, egocentricity, pride, and arrogance, yet in the midst of these negative vices, people pride themselves as Christians or followers of the Lord Jesus Christ.

We go to Church every Sunday, listen to the Message of Truth, partake of the Lord's Supper, and even preach the Message of Truth, yet the Truth has no impact upon our lives. Unfortunately, the misconception, misunderstand, misrepresentation, misappropriation and mistranslation of Scriptures have now turned the simplistic presentation of our faith into a religion of corruption, manipulation, hypocrisy, lies, envy, hate, and deception; thus, neglecting the "pillar of love", which is the bedrock of our great faith.

"What Would You Do If You Were Made A God For A Day?" explains the true meaning of Christianity and the foundation on which it stands. This little book analyzes the essence and mystery of love and brings you face-to-face with the Truth.

"What Would You Do If You Were Made A God For A Day?" will put you on the spot, compel you to examine your life inside and out, and eventually position you to where you belong, as a child of God. This is a life-transforming book that will no doubt develop your Christian character, inspire you to live a selfless life of love, and take you to another level in life.

Chapter One

The Understanding of Being a God

Being a god is something that most believers do not really desire, but the fact of the matter is that in most cases, we are made gods by the Almighty God, and we don't even recognize such a great divine honor. This is because we are either too busy with ourselves or too insensitive to recognize such a spiritual honor and the responsibilities that go along with it.

Before going any further, it is important we comprehend in this regard that we, as human beings, are the image or reflection of the Creator (the Almighty God), which indicates that each and everyone of us possess some attributes or characteristics of the Most High God. Unfortunately, our godly attributes or characteristics become corrupted whenever we allow our ego or flesh to dominate or suppress our spirit-man. Evidently, the Book of Genesis reveals that we are created in the image and likeness of our Creator (the Almighty God), which also proves that we are a representation of the Creator (the Almighty God) here on earth. It is sad how some of our brothers and sisters in the scientific world are of the perception that there is no God nor were we created by God. Nevertheless, the simple logic is that everything that is made must have a maker, and everything that is created must have a creator. Nothing just happens out of the blue; rather, something must make something happen. Genesis 1:27 says, *"So God created man in his own image, in the image of God created he him; male and female created he them."* In the above Scripture, the Hebrew word for **created** is **bara**, meaning to select, to choose, etc.

The question is, "What did God select?" When you read the above Scripture, you will notice that it says, **"male** and **female** created he **them"**, but at this time, only Adam was created and Eve was not yet created. Genesis 2:18-24 tells us how God put Adam to sleep, took one of his ribs, and made the woman (Eve). This means that Adam was created alone, and not with anybody else. If this is so, then why was Adam being referred to in the plural form, as **"them"** or **"male and female"**? The answer is simple, spirits are beings with dual sexes, but are bodiless and colorless. This is why God, being a Spirit, belongs to all races, tongues, and people of the world.

In Genesis 1:27, what God did was to select (to distinguish) the spirit of Adam out of Himself during the creation of Adam. The biological evidence of this profound truth can be seen in people who are born with dual sexes (both male and female organs). Genesis 1:27 also tells us that man was created in the **"image"** of God. The Hebrew word for **image,** as used in the above Scripture, is **tselem**, meaning a representative figure, a resemblance, a reflection, etc. This tells us that an image is a representation or resemblance of something, but it is not that very thing. For example, when you look into the mirror, what you see in it is your image and not you yourself. This is why when you take a gun and shoot at your image in the mirror, you wouldn't get hurt. It is not you who has been shot; rather, it is only your reflection or representation (image). Likewise, we are a representation of the Almighty God; in other words, we are spirits who have been embodied in physical flesh to achieve God's plan and purpose in the physical world. However, we are not **"God"** Himself, and we can never be like (identical to) the Almighty God. John 4:24 teaches that God is a Spirit, and so is His image. Therefore, if God is a Spirit, who created man in **"His"** image and likeness, then it means that which He created in His image must as well be a spirit. This indicates that the creation which took place according to Genesis 1:27 was no doubt spiritual, and not physical. The physicality or materiality of man came into being when God took the dirt of the earth, covered up the Spirit of Man, and made him into a physical being – Genesis 2:7, *"And the Lord God formed man of the dust of the ground, and breathed into his nostrils the breath of life; and man became a living soul."* In this Scripture, the Hebrew word for formed is **yatsar**, meaning to mold into a form, especially as a potter molds clay; to squeeze into a shape, etc. This no doubt proves that we were first created as a spirit being, then later formed (molded) into a physical being. This is why, when a man dies, his spirit returns to the Most High God who gave it, while his lifeless body (mortal remains) returns to the ground (dust) from whence it came – Genesis 3:19, *"In the sweat of thy face shalt thou eat bread, till thou return unto the ground; for out of it wast thou taken: for dust thou art, and unto dust shalt thou return."* The above reveals that we are smaller gods who are trapped in physical bodies. Our god-like attributes or characteristics can be adequately manifested when we embrace the mystical teachings of the Lord Jesus Christ and give expression to them. In fact, the Apostle Paul was trying to simplify the profundity of the above when he said to the Corinthians that God dwells in us – 2 Corinthians 6:16, *"And what agreement hath the temple of God with idols? For ye are the temple of the living God; as God hath said,* **I will dwell in them, and walk in them; and I will be their God, and they shall be my people.***"*

Meanwhile, in order to better understand the subject, it is important that we lucidly understand who is a god and what characteristics make someone a god. A god is a being who is perceived as supernatural, immortal, and having special powers over the lives and affairs of people and the course of nature; an image that is worshipped; a person or thing deified (to glorify, exalt, or adore in an extreme way, or to idolize) or excessively honored and admired, etc. A god is also a title given to superior or supreme spirits, which indicates that besides the Almighty God, there are smaller "gods", including some human beings (you and me). However, due to the monotheistical belief on which our faith (Christianity) was founded, we are not to worship other gods or man, except for the Living and True God of Heaven and Earth. This indicates that smaller gods are not to be worshipped or adored, but they can be respected and honored for the works or services that God does through them. This also means it is possible that God can make a man a god, depending upon the circumstances or event. For example, when the Most High God was about to emancipate His people from Egypt and perform great wonders, He told His servant Moses that He had made him a god to Pharaoh – Exodus 7:1, "And the Lord said unto Moses, See, **I have made thee a god to Pharaoh**: *and Aaron thy brother shall be thy prophet."* It is obvious that God made Moses a god because of the power, virtues, and authority He bestowed upon him and the manner in which He used him to emancipate His people. Moses was also a god to his people because he was used by the Almighty God to meet his people at the point of their needs.

The psalmist David wrote in the Psalms about how God called the believers gods among all His children, irrespective of the fact that we will all die like men and fall like one of the princes – Psalm 82:6-7, *"I have said, Ye are gods; and all of you are children of the most High. But ye shall die like men, and fall like one of the princes."* Also, the Lord Jesus Christ, contending with the envious Pharisees over His Divine Sonship or right as the Son of the Living God, made reference to Psalm 82:6, stating that it is no robbery or controversy if He is called the Son of God because God Himself called us gods – John 10:33-36, *"The Jews answered him, saying, 'For a good work we stone thee not; but for blasphemy; and because that thou, being a man, makest thyself God'. Jesus answered them, 'Is it not written in your law, I said, Ye are gods? If he called them gods, unto whom the word of God came, and the scripture cannot be broken; Say ye of him, whom the Father hath sanctified, and sent into the world, Thou blasphemest; because I said, I am the Son of God?'"* In support of the above, when the Almighty God promised the salvation of Israel, He also promised to make them gods to their neighbors and enemies, such that people would bow before them, see God in them, and call them "gods" – Isaiah 45:14-17, *"Thus saith the Lord, The labour of Egypt, and merchandise of Ethiopia and of the Sabeans, men of stature, shall come over unto thee, and they shall be thine: they shall come after thee;* **in chains they shall come over, and they shall fall down unto thee, they shall make supplication unto thee, saying, Surely God is in thee; and there is none else, there is no God. Verily thou art a God that hidest thyself, O God of Israel, the Saviour.** *They shall be ashamed, and also confounded, all of them: they shall go to confusion together that are makers of idols. But Israel shall be saved in the Lord with an everlasting salvation: ye shall not be ashamed nor confounded world without end."* As a matter of fact, it is only the Spirit of the Most High God that can make a believer a god. For example, when the prophecy of the birth of our Lord Jesus Christ was told, it stated that a virgin would conceive, bring forth a son, and call his name Emmanuel, meaning "God is with us" – Matthew 1:23, *" Behold, a virgin shall be with child, and shall bring forth a son, and they shall call his name Emmanuel, which being interpreted is, God with us."*

"God being with us" simply indicates the presence of God in our midst. When the Spirit of God is upon a person, it means that the presence of the Almighty God is with that person; therefore, he or she is a god who possesses some divine attributes, power, and authority. The Apostle John was trying to express this fact when he wrote in 1 John 4:4, **"Ye are of God, little children, and have overcome them: because greater is he that is in you, than he that is in the world."** This Scripture makes it clear that when the Spirit of God, through our Lord Jesus Christ, dwells in us, automatically, we are possessed with some divine virtues, powers, and authority, which makes us greater than any negative powers that are in the world, irrespective of the trials that we may go through. This explains why the Apostle Paul said that we are more than conquerors, in spite of our trials – Romans 8:35-39, *"Who shall separate us from the love of Christ? shall tribulation, or distress, or persecution, or famine, or nakedness, or peril, or sword? As it is written, For thy sake we are killed all the day long; we are accounted as sheep for the slaughter. Nay,* **in all these things we are more than conquerors through him that loved us.** *For I am persuaded, that neither death, nor life, nor angels, nor principalities, nor powers, nor things present, nor things to come, Nor height, nor depth, nor any other creature, shall be able to separate us from the love of God, which is in Christ Jesus our Lord."* The love of God makes us one with Him. This oneness is inseparable and can cause God to go to any lengths to bless and protect us. The truth is, if we do not recognize the power or the god in us, there is no way that we will be able to exercise the power that is within us. What gives recognition to the power of god that is within us are humility, faith, obedience, God-fear, and consistent prayer and fasting.

When Paul and Barnabas fled to Lycaonia, God justified that His Spirit was within them by performing great signs and miracles through their ministration; thus, making them gods to people. However, due to the polytheistical idol worship mentality of the people, they misunderstood the power of God and thought that Paul and Barnabas were their demonic idols (gods), Jupiter and Mercurius, who had come to visit them in human form. When Paul and Barnabas noticed their ignorance, they quickly prevented the people from worshipping them by warning them to accept the Lord Jesus Christ as Lord and Personal Savior and to worship only the Most High God of Heaven and Earth – Acts 14:5-18, *"And when there was an assault made both of the Gentiles, and also of the Jews with their rulers, to use them despitefully, and to stone them, They were ware of it, and fled unto Lystra and Derbe, cities of Lycaonia, and unto the region that lieth round about: And there they preached the gospel. And there sat a certain man at Lystra, impotent in his feet, being a cripple from his mother's womb, who never had walked: The same heard Paul speak: who stedfastly beholding him, and perceiving that he had faith to be healed, Said with a loud voice, Stand upright on thy feet. And he leaped and walked. And when the people saw what Paul had done, they lifted up their voices, saying in the speech of Lycaonia, The gods are come down to us in the likeness of men. And they called Barnabas, Jupiter; and Paul, Mercurius, because he was the chief speaker. Then the priest of Jupiter, which was before their city, brought oxen and garlands unto the gates, and would have done sacrifice with the people. Which when the apostles, Barnabas and Paul, heard of, they rent their clothes, and ran in among the people, crying out, And saying, Sirs, why do ye these things? We also are men of like passions with you, and preach unto you that ye should turn from these vanities unto the living God, which made heaven, and earth, and the sea, and all things that are therein: Who in times past suffered all nations to walk in their own ways. Nevertheless he left not himself without witness, in that he did good, and gave us rain from heaven, and fruitful seasons, filling our hearts with food and gladness. And with these sayings scarce restrained they the people, that they had not done sacrifice unto them."*

The above teaches that when the Almighty God makes us gods before men, we ought to humble ourselves and give God all the glory or else we will provoke the anger of God, which will unleash darkness across our path – Jeremiah 13:16, *"Give glory to the Lord your God, before he cause darkness, and before your feet stumble upon the dark mountains, and, while ye look for light, he turn it into the shadow of death, and make it gross darkness."* Also, Isaiah 48:11 says, *"For mine own sake, even for mine own sake, will I do it: for how should my name be polluted? and I will not give my glory unto another."* We saw the effect of the above when the Most High God made Herod a god before his people. Unfortunately, he was too full of himself and allowed pride and arrogance to grab hold of him. Hence, he forgot to be mindful of giving God the glory, so God, in His anger, struck him with death. He decomposed immediately and was then eaten by worms. This tells you how our pride and arrogance can sometimes cause us to rob God of His glory – Acts 12:21-25, *"And upon a set day Herod, arrayed in royal apparel, sat upon his throne, and made an oration unto them. And the people gave a shout, saying, It is the voice of a god, and not of a man. And immediately the angel of the Lord smote him, because he gave not God the glory: and he was eaten of worms, and gave up the ghost. But the word of God grew and multiplied. And Barnabas and Saul returned from Jerusalem, when they had fulfilled their ministry, and took with them John, whose surname was Mark."* Today, it is unfortunate to recognize that in this contemporary world, God is still striking people spiritually for not giving Him the glory.

Chapter Two

Divine Encounter

The temptation of being a god in the flesh can lead to pride, arrogance, disobedience, evil, and lack of submission to God and His Holy Spirit. We saw this in the Book of Genesis when the desire to be a god led Eve to disobey God; thus, making her to eat the forbidden fruit – Genesis 3:5, "For God doth know that in the day ye eat thereof, then your eyes shall be opened, and ye shall be as gods, knowing good and evil." The truth is, only humility, obedience, faith, the fear of the Living God, the acceptance of the Lord Jesus Christ, and the empowerment of God's Holy Spirit can make us gods before our fellow human beings. For example, most Asians are knowledgeable of the fact that due to the divine nature of God, who exists within them, they are gods. Therefore, they are able to do exploits or great things without a relationship with the Lord Jesus Christ, without the Holy Spirit, and without the application of the good virtues of life. Although these people may attempt to recognize the god within them and give expression to it by developing their environment and doing great things, this does not necessarily mean that they are on the right path of life spiritually. We must not be ignorant in recognizing that the devil is deceptive and that since the beginning of time, he has always endeavored to interfere with our relationship with the Almighty God by corrupting our beliefs, our faith, and our lives, as a whole. We saw this when he corrupted Herod, through the spirit of pride, arrogance, and inner self-dependency, which prevented him from giving God His glory. Therefore, if any man or preacher should teach you about being possessed with inner powers and does not teach you to reverence the Holy Spirit, the Lord Jesus Christ, and the Almighty God, he is not of God. Such a man is leading you on the path of Satanism and hell-fire; therefore, he must be condemned and repudiated.

Notwithstanding, if the Almighty God should make you a god and give you all of the divine powers and virtues that He possesses for just a day, what would you do? The following story tells how two strong, faithful, and dedicated believers, who have been praying faithfully for breakthrough and divine intervention in their lives encountered God's Angel and were challenged with this question.

One Saturday morning, after praying for seven long years, Bill and Jack decided to go for a seven-day retreat in the countryside of their home state, with the hope that the silence of the countryside would afford them an opportunity to hear the voice of God very distinctly. At the end of their seven-day retreat, just when they were about to break their fast, the Angel of the Lord appeared to them in human form and said, "…The Lord has seen your tears and has felt your pain, so He has sent me to bless the two of you, according to the desires of your hearts. However, before I bless the two of you, there is a question that each of you will have to answer. Bill, you are the first person that I am going ask, and the question goes like this – 'If the Almighty God should make you a god and bestow upon you all of His divine powers, authority, and virtues for just a day, what would you do?'" Bill held his peace and kept silent for a while. Later, with a deep sense of excitement and self-confidence, he breathed out his fear and said to the Angel, "If the Almighty God should make me a god and give me all His powers and virtues for just a day, first, I would build a big church for the Lord and decorate it with gold, inside and out. Second, I would get some vans and buses for evangelism and the running of the ministry. Third, I would get a mansion and a few nice cars and SUVs for my family and me, so that the glory of God could be reflected in our lives. Fourth, I would help all the poor people in my church and build a shelter for the homeless. Last, I would deal with all my enemies once and for all, so that they wouldn't bother me anymore, and I wouldn't need to pray about them ever again." The Angel nodded speechlessly and later said, "Well done, Bill, it shall be as you have spoken." He then turned toward Jack and asked him the same question that he had asked Bill. With a deep sense of humility, Jack stared into the face of the Angel and said, "Sir, this is a very difficult question; however, I'll try to give you my honest and realistic answer. If the Almighty God should make me a god and bestow upon me all His divine power, authority, and virtues, first, I would worship Him and give Him thanks and adoration for such a great honor and opportunity to share His burdens. Second, I would forgive all my enemies and give them a second chance because God did the same for me. In fact, it is because of God's second chance that I am still alive today. Third, I would heal the sicknesses and diseases of all the faithful believers who are sick and have been praying to God for healing. Fourth, I would answer the prayers of all the faithful believers, who have been praying to God for a specific request, including fruit of the womb, financial breakthrough, traveling mercies, etc. Fifth, I would make all the poor, but faithful believers, who are homeless, to be middle-class and give each of them a home of their own. Sixth, I would empower the faithful church with anointing, power, and all the necessary material resources in order to do aggressive evangelism for the Kingdom of God because the time is near for the coming of the Lord. Last, I would grant my personal requests, according to the will of God for my life." The Angel of God smiled, and smiled, and smiled again. He nodded and said to Jack, "Son, the Lord God Almighty has honored all that you have said and holds you in high esteem. He has already answered your prayers. Go in peace, for you are highly favored and blessed!" After the Angel of the Lord had blessed both Jack and Bill, He promised to visit them in seven years.

Henceforth, Jack was blessed and favored from then onward. One month after the publication of his books, he became a millionaire. He dedicated his entire life to God and to the service of humanity. Jack initiated a program to help people out of poverty. He often visited the homeless with gifts and assisted in providing shelter for some. Also, Jack often visited the sick in the hospital, especially people he didn't know, and he paid the hospital bill for all those who could not afford it. He even comforted those who were sad, distressful, and felt hopeless in life by praying with them and providing them with every assistance needed. In addition, Jack visited the prison regularly to minister to those who are incarcerated. Jack's entire life became very preoccupied with sharing the burdens of God. Most of all, Jack fulfilled every word that he had told the Angel of the Lord. He consistently appreciated the Almighty God and walked before Him daily with a heart of worship and thanksgiving. He forgave all his known enemies and gave them a second chance in life, considering that the Lord Jesus Christ did the same for him on Calvary over 2,000 years ago. Jack was also endowed with the gift of healing, of which he used appropriately to the glory of God, and not for his pride, ego, and fame. He became a good friend of the poor and a lover of sinners. His life of humility and simplicity gravitated all categories of people to him, particularly the poor and others who have lost hope in life. In fact, he strongly warned his staff, especially his personal secretary that they must allow anyone who desires to see him to be given immediate access to him, in particular, the poorest of the poor, irrespective of his/her appearance or physical condition.

In the case of Bill, it was a bit different, despite the fact that he kept his promise to the Angel. He built a beautiful church with a gold altar. He purchased vans and buses for evangelism, as promised. He even built a huge mansion for himself and bought himself a fleet of cars. He also distributed food and clothing to the poor every Christmas; however, he would publicize it on the radio and television, so that the world would see him as a "good giver". In reality, Bill was only concerned with fame, publicity, and making a name for himself, but in the end, he was robbing God of His glory. In fact, he had pictures of himself displayed inside and outside of his church, as well as large billboards of himself along the principal streets of the city, as if he was a politician running a political campaign.

Chapter Three

The Blessings, The Pride, and The Temptation

$\mathcal{M}$eanwhile, in the seventh year of their blessings, the Lord Jesus Christ Himself decided to come down to earth and visit both Bill and Jack when the young men least expected. He first got a hold of Bill's office number, then proceeded to dial it. The phone rang distinctly and within a span of three seconds, Bill's personal secretary answered the phone in a very friendly tone of voice and said, "Hi, this is Bishop Bill Jones Ministry, may I help you?"

"Yes, I'm Mr. Hill, and I would like to speak with Bishop Bill Jones," said Mr. Hill.

"Mr. Hill, do you have an appointment with Bishop Bill Jones?" asked Bill's personal secretary.

"No, but he's aware that I should be meeting him at this particular time," replied Mr. Hill.

"Where are you calling from and what is the name of your company or ministry?" inquired Bill's personal secretary.

"I'm just a homeless man who needs help from the Bishop," responded Mr. Hill.

"I'm sorry, Mr. Hill but Bishop did not give me a directive concerning you, and I don't think it's possible for you to talk to him today, due to his very busy schedule. However, if you need any assistance, you may visit our church and someone will be available to talk to you. We are located at 700 Grace Avenue," said Bill's secretary.

"Well, I'll try to visit your church, if I can. Good talking to you and have a nice day," concluded Mr. Hill, as he hung up the phone.

A few minutes after Mr. Hill hung up the phone, he picked it up again, but this time, he dialed Bill's cell number. After three rings, he answered and said, "Hi, this is Bishop Bill Jones, may I help you?"

"Yes, please, I'm Mr. Hill, a homeless man from across the street. We may not know each other, but I heard about your good works in the community and decided to ask you for some assistance," replied Mr. Hill.

"First of all, thank you for your compliment. Unfortunately, we don't help people just like that. We have to know whom they are, where they're from, and so on. Besides, anybody can claim to be a homeless person; therefore, if you're really in need of help, you may visit our church at 700 Grace Avenue, and someone will be there to talk to you. By the way, how'd you get my cell number?" asked Bill.

"Well, I got your cell number from someone I didn't even know," answered Mr. Hill.

"Well, that's not very important. Unfortunately, I am in the middle of a meeting. I'm afraid I'll have to hang up now," Bill interrupted.

Bent on proving the character of Bill, Mr. Hill visited his church on the following Sunday, wearing his usual very old, dirty, and shabby-looking clothes. When he arrived at the church, the beautifully dressed ushers wouldn't allow him into the building, but later, a young man intervened. He told the ushers to disregard the physical appearance of Mr. Hill and allow him into the church; hence, it is the House of God. Surprisingly, the ushers listened to the young man and reluctantly allowed Mr. Hill to enter the church; however, they ushered him to an empty seat at the rear of the sanctuary, where he quietly sat.

Mr. Hill observed all their hypocrisy during the service. At the end of the service, Mr. Hill immediately fought his way through the crowd and met Bill (the Bishop) in person, despite all the hindrances and opposition coming from church workers, ushers, and even close friends and relatives of Bill.

"Can I talk to you for a minute, Bishop?" asked Mr. Hill.

"I will see you later," replied Bill, as he walked away from Mr. Hill and went into his office.

Mr. Hill never gave up; in fact, he forced his way into the lobby and waited patiently until Bill had finished talking to all of the rich, well-dressed, and influential members of his church. He then proceeded to Bill's personal secretary and said, "I'm the only person left, so can I see your Bishop?"

"Sir, I'm sorry, but Bishop does not have an appointment with you. If you need any assistance, I can refer you to someone who can help you," responded Bill's personal secretary.

"I may not have an appointment with your Bishop, but it is imperative that I see him. Can I please?" pleaded Mr. Hill.

Bill's personal secretary bowed her head in silence for a while but later stood up and told Mr. Hill, "Excuse me, Sir. I'll be back."

She then entered Bill's office. "Bishop, I'm sorry to bother you, but there's a homeless man sitting in the lobby who is insisting on seeing you. He's been here for almost two hours now. What should I tell him?" asked Bill's personal secretary.

"You know the rules. I'm tired of repeating your job description to you. You know what to do. If he needs prayer, take him to Pastor James or if he needs food or some sort of assistance, take him to the welfare department. Why does he need to see me?" replied Bill.

Bill's personal secretary returned from his office only to tell Mr. Hill that He couldn't see Bill. He told the young lady thanks and politely walked out of Bill's office disappointed, irrespective of the fact that she attempted to take Him to see the junior pastors and those in charge of the welfare department of the church. The fact is that he really wanted to see the Bishop, and not some other pastors. Two weeks after Mr. Hill's visitation to Bill's office, his wife and three children were returning from summer camp when a truck ran into them and killed the four of them instantly.

When the tragic news of the death of Bill's family reached him, he was so devastated that he nearly gave up the ghost. He went into his prayer closet and asked God, "Why?" In the midst of his prayer and agony, the Lord Jesus Christ appeared to Bill in the form of Mr. Hill. Bill immediately recognized Him in the same old, ripped-up, shabby clothes He wore when He approached him in the church, but this time, he realized that this filthy-looking man who has appeared to him was no other than the Savior of the World, the Lord Jesus Christ Himself. Soon after his eyes were opened spiritually, the Lord Jesus Christ took his real form and said to Bill, "It is too late. You know Son, in some cases, VIP may not always mean Very Important Person, but in a world of fools, greed, and selfishness, VIP may also mean Very Ignorant Person. The truth is, I knew of your pride, arrogance, egocentricity, and self-righteousness long before you were even conceived in your mother's womb. I tried to have access to you on three occasions, but your pride, arrogance, self-righteousness, and egocentricity just wouldn't allow me to have access to you. You denied me your presence, so now I have denied you the presence of the people you love the most in this life. Appearing to you as Mr. Hill, I wanted you to be a god to me, but you were too busy to be my god. Therefore, I cannot be a god to you, and I will not hear you at this time. You must remember that the same God of the rich is the same God of the poor. He hears everybody, but it is only time that concludes man's efforts." The Lord Jesus Christ went further and said the below poem, ***"His Thoughts Are Not Ours"***:

> *If you think that God is blind that He cannot see;*
> *His watching eyes are ever open,*
> *running to and fro throughout the earth,*
> *to protect His children at all times.*
>
> *If you think that God is deaf and cannot hear;*
> *His listening and omniscient ears are ever attentive*
> *to hear all languages and respond to all cries.*
>
> *If you think that God is crippled*
> *so that He cannot walk with you;*
> *His omnipresent legs are everywhere*
> *at the same time to gently walk with you.*
>
> *If you think that God is so careless*

that He cannot help in your situation;
His helping and omnipotent Hands
are ever open to give you a big push in life.

If you think that God's telephone line is blocked
so that you cannot call Him;
His line is always open
seven days a week, twenty-four hours a day,
and twelve months a year,
to receive calls from every soul in any part of the earth,
because God doesn't pay bills.

His thoughts are not ours.

At the conclusion of the above poem, the Lord Jesus Christ told Bill the following sad words, "In fact, by this time next year, you will join your family, and strangers will enjoy your labor." After saying those words to Bill, the Lord Jesus Christ disappeared and left him weeping.

Chapter Four

Walking the Heart of God

$\mathscr{A}$ few days later, a hungry homeless man was spotted by the side of the road all alone. As he slowly walked down the road, he became increasingly famished, so he decided to stop moving cars to beg for spare change or loose cash in order to get himself some food to eat. He attempted to stop the first car that drove by, but the driver drove passed him with terrific speed, not even recognizing him as a human being in need in the dead of winter. The second car also passed him in the same manner as the first. When he attempted to stop the third car, it passed him, but later stopped. The driver reversed, rolled down his window, and said to Mr. Black, "Where're you going? Can I give you a lift?"

"Thanks! I need a ride, but I'm also very hungry and very cold," replied Mr. Black.

"Come on in!" exclaimed the driver of the car enthusiastically.

Mr. Black happily got into the car, and they drove off. As they proceeded, the driver of the car introduced himself, "I'm Jack, and what's your name?"

"I'm Mr. Black, a hungry homeless man with no family and nowhere to go," responded Mr. Black.

With a deep sense of pity and concern, Jack told Mr. Black, "As long as God remains gracious unto me, you won't be a homeless man anymore." He further told Mr. Black, "Man's condition is not interminable. This is why mankind must always endeavor to help his fellow human at all cost. A man's condition does not conclude his life, neither does it determine his end; rather, it is just another remarkable page of his life that will soon be turned over. Besides, life does not end in trials; rather, it begins afresh."

"What do you mean?" asked Mr. Black.

"You must understand that what a man speaks out of his mouth determines what he knows and understands. Likewise, what a man professes about God determines what he knows and understands about God. Well, first, I am taking you to a restaurant called the **Watering Mouth** to get you some hot food to eat, then I will take you to my homeless shelter right on the outskirts of the city," replied Jack, with a huge grin on his face.

After a few minutes' drive, both Jack and Mr. Black arrived at the **Watering Mouth**, where Jack ordered a hot meal for Mr. Black. When Mr. Black was finished eating, Jack requested the bill and paid for Mr. Black's food. As they were leaving the restaurant, Jack left a $50.00 tip for the waitress, as well as his name card with a note, inviting her to visit his church on Sunday. From the **Watering Mouth**, Jack and Mr. Black then proceeded to a department store, where Jack bought Mr. Black some of the basic necessities, including a toothbrush, a tube of toothpaste, a pair of sneakers, a winter jacket, a bath towel, etc. After leaving the department store, they went to a nearby boutique, where Jack bought Mr. Black some nice clothes and shoes that can be worn for Sunday church service, as well as for any other important occasion. When they finally finished shopping, they then went to Jack's homeless shelter, of which he called "Jesus Christ's Home of Love". When they arrived at the shelter, Jack introduced Mr. Black to the staff as "his good friend and special guest" and ordered that He should be given whatever He wants. After arrangements were made for Mr. Black at the shelter, Jack inspected Mr. Black's room, as well as made sure that He was treated well and was very comfortable. Jack later embraced Mr. Black, prayed with him, and left for his home.

While en-route to his home, Jack spotted a man who was badly beaten and was about to be robbed by a gang of five young men. He immediately pulled over and ran to the rescue of this man who appeared to be a well-off businessman.

"Police! Don't move! Put your hands up!" exclaimed Jack, as he held onto his right side, pretending to be holding a pistol with his right hand, while holding his wallet in his left hand, as if he was identifying himself. Jack continued, "Drop your weapons before I blow your brains out!"

Upon hearing the order of Jack, the five young men immediately halted their criminal act and held their hands up.

"You guys should be in school at this time. Get out of here before I put you all behind bars," threatened Jack.

The young men absconded, leaving the beaten and wounded man lying on the ground, as he bled from his facial wounds.

"I'm sorry that this had to happen to you. Can I take you to the hospital?" asked Jack.

"No! I'm fine, but thank you very much! I can make it there. My car is parked just right there in the parking lot," responded the wounded man.

Jack then helped the wounded man from the ground and escorted him to his car. Before the wounded man could drive off to the hospital, he said to Jack, "God bless you and thank you ever so much! You are an angel who was sent to rescue me!"

"God bless you too, and I wish you a speedy recovery. If you ever need anything, here is my card. Please feel free to contact me at anytime," Jack responded.

"Thanks for the card! By the way, are you a real cop because I didn't see a badge?" asked the wounded man.

"Well, not really, I only took the risk to save your life. Besides, I'm a cop for Jesus," replied Jack.

"That's a serious risk that can only be taken by people of faith. God bless you again and have a great day," said the wounded man.

As the wounded man drove off, Jack stood by watching his car, after which, he finally drove off to his house.

At approximately 11 o'clock the next morning, Jack went back to the shelter to check on Mr. Black and the others. He met Mr. Black and told him that if he wouldn't mind, he would love to introduce him to his family. Mr. Black accepted Jack's invitation and immediately followed him to his house. When they arrived at Jack's house, Jack's wife, daughter, and two sons warmly welcomed Mr. Black into their home. In fact, Jack's wife told Mr. Black that their guest room was available and insisted that Mr. Black stay with them for "as long as he wishes". Jack and his children also supported the decision, which was made hours earlier. Mr. Black tried to turn down the offer, but Jack and his family insisted. Eventually, they all drove back to the shelter, collected all of Mr. Black's belongings, and brought them to their home. Mr. Black was now living with Jack and his family in their guest bedroom downstairs.

Meanwhile, Jack remained consistent in his regular hospital and prison visitations, irrespective of his position as overseer of a megachurch. He was also consistent in his regular door-to-door and street evangelism that were done with members of his church. All of these things were carefully monitored by Mr. Black. On one of his regular hospital visits, Jack came across a man who was dying of heart disease and needed emergency surgery in order to survive. Unfortunately, this man was very poor and his surgery was very costly. When Jack met this man in his hospital room, he wept, especially after seeing the deplorable state of his health. He immediately prayed with him and asked, "Sir, what's wrong?"

"I have been diagnosed with heart disease, and the doctor told me that I must undergo surgery in three days or else I will die," the sick man replied. "Unfortunately, I have no insurance, and I don't know what to do or where to go."

Upon hearing this sad news from the sick man, Jack sympathized and immediately ran to meet the doctor in charge. He inquired about the cost of the sick man's surgery and was told that the out-of-pocket cost was $120,000.00. That was a lot of money to spend on just one man's health, but at the same time, that man may have been the one lost sheep amongst hundreds who needed to live in order to declare the goodness and glory of the Most High God.

Being convicted by the Holy Spirit and at the same time suppressing his ego, Jack quickly ran down the stairs, went into his car, drew out his checkbook from his briefcase, and wrote a check for $125,000.00. He went back upstairs, handed the check over to the doctor and said, "Here's a check for Mr. Mark's surgery. I included an extra $5,000.00 in it for his provisions, medications, and special care.

Just in case you need anything extra, please contact me immediately. Here's my card."

With shock and amazement, the doctor received the check and said, "This is strange! You don't know this man from anywhere, yet you are spending so much money on him."

Jack's reply was simple and to the point, "True wealth is not measured by what a man gathers, but how much he distributes."

Within a span of 30 minutes, the doctor scheduled Mr. Mark's (the sick man's) surgery for the next morning at 10am. Jack went back to Mr. Mark and told him that God has taken care of everything, and it is well. He further told Mr. Mark, "By the grace of God, tomorrow your surgery will be done, and it's going to be OK. By the way, excuse me for asking you this, but do you have a place to stay after you have been discharged from here?"

"First of all, I must say thank you very much for your kindness and generosity towards me. You didn't have to do this. I just can't understand why you went above and beyond to do this for me. Words are inadequate in expressing my gratitude. However, two weeks prior to my sickness, I was kicked out of my apartment for not being able to meet my rental obligations. Soon afterwards, I fell off on the street one afternoon, and when I regained consciousness, I found myself lying on this hospital bed. So at the moment, I don't have a home," cried Mr. Mark.

Jack paused for a while and later said the below words of encouragement to Mr. Mark:

"He never leaves me alone,
because I am His child.
I am helpless and empty without Him.
But when He's around,
I am strong.

Whenever He touches me,
there is always a change in my life.

Whenever I'm attacked and
find myself in the midst of panic and battle,
He becomes my Shield of Faith,
Breastplate of Righteousness,
and Sword of the Spirit.
Whenever I'm misled and
find myself in the midst of chaos and temptation,
He becomes my Helmet of Salvation,
Belt of Truth, and Shoes of Peace.

In life's journey,
He never leaves me behind.
He is always by my side,
and at the forefront of my life.

Whenever He leaves me hungry;
it is for my strength and
not for my starvation.

Whenever I cry;
it is for my joy and
not for my sorrow.

Whenever I'm in danger;
it is for my courage and
not for my defeat.

Whenever I'm in trial;
it is for my blessing in my season and
not for my shame.

Whenever I labor;
it is for my comfort and
not for my suffering.
Whenever I'm lifted up;
it is for my joy and laughter and
not for my boast and pride.

In the midst of frustration and uncertainty,
my faith is tested and
my focus keeps steady on Him.

He never leaves me alone."

At the conclusion of the above poetic words, Jack said to Mr. Mark, "Remember, just as He never leaves me alone, He also will never leave you alone. By the way, would you like to be at my shelter when you are out of here?" he asked.

"Sure, I would, if God allows!" answered Mr. Mark.

"Take my card so that when your surgery is done, you can give me a call, and I'll come to get you," said Jack with a great big smile on his face.

Two days later, Jack received a call on his cell phone. It was Dr. Luke, calling from Restoration Hospital.

"Hello, this is Jack, may I help you?"

"I'm Dr. Luke, calling from Restoration Hospital. You were here two days ago, and you gave me your name card, ordering me to call you if I needed to do so," explained Dr. Luke.

"Oh yes, I remember. Is everything OK? How's my good friend, Mr. Mark? How did the surgery go?" asked Jack.

"Well, this is why I am calling you. Unfortunately, there were some complications during the surgery, and I'm afraid that your friend Mark did not make it. We did everything we could, but we just couldn't save him," reported Dr. Luke in a very soft tone of voice.

Upon hearing this very sad news, Jack was flabbergasted for a few seconds, then began to reflect on the loss of Mr. Mark. It was not the loss of money that concerned Jack; rather, his grief and pain were due to the fact that he had just lost a soul, of whom he had desperately wanted to see live in order to glorify God.

"Hello, hello, are you there, Mr. Jack?" interrupted Dr. Luke.

"I'm sorry, I'm still on the line. I'll be with you in less than an hour," responded Jack.

In seconds, Jack was in his car, headed towards Restoration Hospital. Within 40 minutes, he arrived at the hospital and met with Dr. Luke. When Jack stood before Dr. Luke, he stared into his eyes speechlessly, as tears rolled down his face. Dr. Luke then embraced Jack and said, "I'm sorry! I'm so sorry!" After which, Dr. Luke escorted Jack to Mr. Mark's empty bed, where Jack's name card and a note from Mr. Mark lay. Dr. Luke picked up the note and card from the bed, then gave them to Jack and said, "He left these for you."

"This is the name card that I gave him just two days ago," said Jack.

He then opened the note which read, "Young man, you are truly God-sent, and I really don't know how to tell you thank you for all that you've done for me. If I make it through the surgery, I'll be glad to stay at your shelter, but in case I don't make it, I'll still be with you in spirit. Continue your good works and may God richly bless and prosper you in all areas of your life. May you and your family never lack in good health, peace, joy, and wealth. Your good old friend, Mark." After reading Mr. Mark's note, Jack wept and later gave Dr. Luke some money for the transfer of Mr. Mark's body to the mortuary.

Chapter Five

God Watches Even the Smallest Things

Meanwhile, Mr. Black kept his eyes opened, as he observed all that was unfolding in Jack's life. The following Sunday was just another cold, wintery Sunday, and it was time for service to commence at "Love Gate Baptist Church". Once the regular Sunday service began, all were seated, as the moderator of the program called Pastor Jack Peters to the pulpit.

"Good morning to you my lovely brothers and sisters, fathers and mothers, and wonderful visitors. We thank the Almighty God for another glorious opportunity to congregate here in His House on this day. The theme of my message this morning is, 'What Is God Benefiting From Your Life?' Well, let us pray."

Right before Jack began preaching his message, the ushers escorted into the church a dirty-looking old man and placed him in an available seat in the front row of the church. The old man, who seemed to be in his late 60's to early 70's, quietly sat as he patiently listened to Jack's wonderful sermon which came from Matthew 22:34-40 and Luke 10:25-37, respectively.

At the conclusion of the service, Jack stood at the entrance of the church, greeting members and visitors alike, including the dirty-looking old man who was visiting the church for the first time. The next day, Jack went to his office as usual and to his surprise, he met the dirty-looking old man, who had visited his church on Sunday, sitting in his lobby in the midst of others who had also come to see him. Jack recognized him and immediately ordered his secretary to escort him into his office, meanwhile apologizing to the others for any inconvenience, due to the change in protocol. After about a minute, the old man was ushered into Jack's office.

"How are you doing, Sir? Is there anything that I can do for you?" asked Jack.

"No Sir, but I just came to let you know that I was truly blessed by your message on Sunday, and I'm ecstatic to tell you that I am now a member of this church," replied the old man.

"Praise God and to Him be all the glory!" exclaimed Jack. He went further and said the below:

*"I am like a feather
and God is like a wind to me.
Wherever He blows me,
there will I go.*

*If He blows me in the water,
there will I swim in hope.*

*If He blows me in the dust,
there will I sit and wait.*

*But if He blows me upwards,
then will I soar like an eagle,
to His glory.*

*He is the Force that makes me move:
the Rain that makes me wet,
and the Sun that makes me dry.*

*He is the Starter of my engine,
and the Driver of my car.*

*He is the Captain of my ship,
and the Pilot of my plane.*

*He is the Director of my destiny,
and the Commander-in-Chief of my life.*

*I am nothing without Him,
but I am everything in Him.*

He is the Accomplisher of my decisions,
and the Implementer of my plans.

He is fearful and unfriendly in my imagination;
but He is loving and merciful in my life.

He is not my imagination,
He is Himself."

At the conclusion of the above poem, **"He Is Not My Imagination, He Is Himself"**, Jack then asked the old man, "Sir, is there anything else I can do for you? Excuse me for asking, but do you have a comfortable home or do you need a hot meal or something?" asked Jack anxiously.

"Trust me, I am more than fine, but if I need anything, I will surely ask you. I must be going now, but I'll see you on Sunday, God willing," replied the old man.

"Before leaving, may I know your name, Sir?" asked Jack.

"Well, you can call me Mr. Smile," the poor old man replied.

"Mr. Smile, here's my card, so just in case you need something or want to talk to somebody, you can call me at anytime, even in the middle of the night," offered Jack.

"How can I call you in the middle of the night, Jack? You have a family and that's not a good thing to do," responded Mr. Smile.

"Well, you don't have to worry about that, which is why I never turn off my phone. The truth is, being a pastor is being a shepherd, and a shepherd never sleeps. He has to always be awake to watch over his flock because you never know when an emergency situation may crop up with a member or a stranger who may need your help. Besides, a pastor is a servant, not a master or boss, and a servant must always be in a position to serve and not play the boss," explained Jack.

Mr. Smile stared at Jack for a while, then said, "I surely will call you. Thank you so much, Pastor and have a wonderful day."

Chapter Six

Sorrowful World, Yet Wonderful World

A week later, Jack decided to give his late friend Mark an honorable funeral and burial. After all arrangements were made, he took custodianship of Mr. Mark's body and organized other homeless from the shelter, as well as members of his congregation for Mr. Mark's funeral on Friday, which was to be held at the Funeral Home Chapel. The next day, Mr. Mark was buried with honor and dignity. Meanwhile, during the burial ceremony of Mr. Mark, Jack spoke very highly of Mr. Mark, as if he had known him for years. After his extensive eulogy, Jack concluded by reading the poem, "Sorrowful World":

> "Sorrowful world, yet wonderful world
> From the unknown, we came into existence
> crossing the paths of business and friendship,
> we meet abruptly in the traffic jam of life
> with so much rage and hatred, we sometimes
> fall apart, and become lifetime enemies
> Sometimes, with so much love and compassion
> we bid farewell and suddenly vanish like smoke,
> never knowing when we shall ever meet again
>
> Sorrowful world, yet, wonderful world
> Life is too short to live without a dream
> but it is more doleful to dream without a hope
> Every life must produce a dream and every dream
> must be let down into the flowing river of hope
> O, how distressful it is to say goodbye,
> having no concept of what the future holds
> How frustrating it is to see oneself so confounded,
> and submerging into the staled memories of yesterday
> O, how laborious it is to omit those good old days,

to ecstatically embrace the stint of the new dawn
Yes! Those wonderful days of joy, peace and glory
Blinded so intensely by the gold of yesterday,
that we neglect to see the precious diamond of today
Living the past is unconsciously repudiating the present,
and deceitfully living a future backwards

O what a sorrowful world, yet, wonderful world
Why ruminate the logic of keeping our candles burning,
when suddenly our flame would be extinguished?
What is our hope, when we can't see any hope?
What is our fate, when thirst and starvation
have mercilessly consumed our energies and speeches
O, what a sorrowful world, yet, wonderful world
When the effulgence of Heaven refuses to be extinguished,
together we shall all be strengthened in power and say,
where there is no hope, there are more hopes,
as long as we exist and are still breathing faithfully
O, so foolish I was to give up so soon,
when the Creator had not given up on me
To the hustlers and the weak, life is a puzzle,
but to the visionary and courageous,
life is a challenge that we all have to face in faith,
and fight our way through it,
whether we are willing or unwilling
O, what a sorrowful world, yet, wonderful world"

When Jack had finished reading the above poem *(Sorrowful World)*, Mr. Mark's coffin was then lowered into the earth and eventually, everyone left the grave site, one after the other.

Three days after the burial of Mr. Mark, Mr. Black fell very ill and vomited all over Jack's living room. Fortunately for Mr. Black, Jack and his family were around when he fell ill and dialed 911 for an ambulance. Irrespective of his ailment, Mr. Black attempted to reach out for the mop in order to mop up his vomit from the wooden floor, but Jack's wife and kids wouldn't allow him. They were more concerned about his health than material things or the beauty of their living room at that moment. Unfortunately, the 911 Ambulance that was en-route to Jack's house had a flat tire, so the driver had to pull over and make arrangements for another.

Notwithstanding, while Jack and his family awaited the arrival of the ambulance, Mr. Black suddenly stood on his feet, regained his strength, and made a miraculous recovery. He then gathered Jack and his family together and said to them, "No need to worry or panic over my condition. I am OK, but it is about time that I leave you guys to go back to my home. It is time to go."

Before Jack could utter a word, Mr. Black interrupted him and said, "Hold your peace and listen. Seven years ago, I promised you that I was going to visit you and your friend, Bill. First, you recognized me at the side of the road when you put me into your car, took me to a restaurant to eat, shopped for me, clothed me, gave me shelter at your center, and eventually brought me into your own home. Second, you visited me at Restoration Hospital, paid for my surgery, and when I went to sleep, you took me to the funeral home and gave me an honorable funeral and burial. Third, I visited your church in rags, but I was warmly welcomed with love and compassion. Also, when I visited your office, you not only recognized me, but you affectionately received me into your office with love, compassion, and honor. Again, I was also very amazed at how you risked your life to save me from those five young men who were about to rob and kill me. Well, one of them is now saved, while the other four were killed in a shootout with a rival gang."

As he spoke to Jack and his family, Mr. Black took the forms of the different personalities of the people whom he had used during his many appearances to Jack. At last, he took the form of the Lord Jesus

Christ and said, "I am the Lord Jesus Christ, and I have come to bless you and your entire family. You and your family are blessed and well-favored above all men. May my peace abide with you forever." As Jack and his family fell flat in worship and tears, the Lord Jesus Christ laid His Hands upon them and later disappeared.

Unlike Bill and his family, who fell short of the grace of God, due to their pride and arrogance, Jack and his family were blessed in health, wealth, and riches above all men. All through their lives, they never got sick, and they had more wealth than any man could ever wish for, but most importantly, their eternity was secured. When it was time for them to meet the Lord in eternity, each of them died at a very old age.

What some people fail to recognize in this life is that appearances can sometimes be deceptive, which is why it is never good to treat a person based on their physical condition or appearance. For example, you cannot call someone dirty if you have no understanding of that person's situation or condition in life. The truth is, poverty has a way of humiliating an individual, stripping that person of his/her dignity, and even making him/her to appear dirty. For instance, if someone is very poor and has no income, it is obvious that most times, that person will appear before people with dirty clothes and body odor. This is because the little money that the individual should use to buy detergent or laundry soap in order to keep his/her clothes clean, would be used on food. I understand this because my family was once in similar circumstances, so I know how it feels to be in such an unfortunate situation.

As I said previously, God judges us from the heart because what has been conceived in the heart is often times spoken by the mouth. This is why our Lord Jesus Christ told the people that it is not what goes into the mouth that corrupts or pollutes (defileth) a man, but what comes out of his mouth – Matthew 15:10-11, *"And he called the multitude, and said unto them, Hear, and understand: Not that which goeth into the mouth defileth a man; but that which cometh out of the mouth, this defileth a man."*

Even though Bill was a faithful, serious-minded, and prayerful Christian who loved the Lord, God was not happy with him, yet he still granted his requests. This is because the spirit of pride, greed, selfishness, and egocentrism was deeply rooted in the behavior of Bill, yet it was covered up with the spirit of religion and self-righteousness. For example, when Bill told the Angel that he would build a big church for God and decorate it with gold inside and out, that reflected his selfishness and pride. This is because a big golden church would mean nothing to God as long as it does not benefit God's people by addressing or meeting their spiritual, material, and physical needs. A big golden church would be meaningless to God as long as God's truth is not adequately preached in it and lives are not spiritually, materially, or physically transformed in it. Likewise, getting vans and buses for evangelism and the running of the ministry would also be of no use to God as long as they are not used for their intended purposes, especially when it comes to transforming lives and conveying believers and non-believers alike to the church.

Also, owning a mansion and a fleet of cars are not the only ways by which God's glory is reflected in our lives. We must realize that God's glory is not only reflected in our material possessions, but it is also reflected in our immaterialized and spiritualized lives. The truth is that it is not what or how much we accumulate in life that reflects God's glory in us, but what is important to God is what we do with what we have accumulated in life. It is the things that we do as believers that reflect God's glory in us, and not that which we accumulate. It is obvious that as human beings, what we accumulate or our material possessions in life are for our own glory and benefit, but the things that we do with them are for the benefit of God and to His glory. Our Lord Jesus Christ was very lucid when He made the Jews to understand that His works are for the honor of His Father in Heaven, and that He came, not to seek His own glory, but for God to be glorified in His works and life – John 8:49-50, *"Jesus answered, I have not a devil; but I honour my Father, and ye do dishonour me. And I seek not mine own glory: there is one that seeketh and judgeth."*

For instance, it is not the power that we possess in us that makes us gods to others, but what we do with the power that we possess within us. Likewise, it is not the precious life that we have in us that matters to God, but what is important to God is what we do with the life that has been graciously given unto us. This explains why when God sees that some people's lives are not benefiting Him or His people materially, spiritually, morally, or physically, He takes them away. Expressing the message of repentance and salvation to the Pharisees, John the Baptist said in Matthew 3:7-10, *"But when he saw many of the Pharisees and Sadducees come to his baptism, he said unto them, O generation of vipers, who hath warned you to flee from the wrath to come? Bring forth therefore fruits meet for repentance: And think not to say within yourselves, We have Abraham to our father: for I say unto you, that God is able of these stones to raise up children unto Abraham. And now also the axe is laid unto the root of the trees: therefore every tree which bringeth not forth good fruit is hewn down, and cast into the fire."*

The above Scripture teaches that if our lives cannot benefit God and affect the lives of others spiritually, morally, materially, financially, etc., then we need not exist. Even the very fig tree that could not provide fruit for the Lord Jesus Christ to eat when He was hungry was later cursed by Jesus – Matthew 21:17-20, *"And he left them, and went out of the city into Bethany; and he lodged there. Now in the morning as he returned into the city, he hungered. And when he saw a fig tree in the way, he came to it, and found nothing thereon, but leaves only, and said unto it, Let no fruit grow on thee henceforward for ever. And presently the fig tree withered away. And when the disciples saw it, they marvelled, saying, How soon is the fig tree withered away!"* Also see Luke 13:6-7.

Nevertheless, it is not wrong to accumulate material possessions in a godly manner, but it is not the basis upon which God's glory is reflected in our lives. The fact is, one does not need material possessions in order for God's glory to be reflected in his or her life. For instance, Moses and his people did not have mansions or a fleet of cars, but after they did that which was required of them by God, God's glory came down upon them – Exodus 40:31-35, *"And Moses and Aaron and his sons washed their hands and their feet thereat: When they went into the tent of the congregation, and when they came near unto the altar, they washed; as the Lord commanded Moses. And he reared up the court round about the tabernacle and the altar, and set up the hanging of the court gate. So Moses finished the work. Then a cloud covered the tent of the congregation, and the glory of the Lord filled the tabernacle. And Moses was not able to enter into the tent of the congregation, because the cloud abode thereon, and the glory of the Lord filled the tabernacle."* Also, see Leviticus 9:23.

Our Lord Jesus Christ, who was glorified by God in His works, death (crucifixion), resurrection, and ascension, never had an earthly mansion or a fleet of cars, yet, the glory of God was reflected in His life inside and out when He was on earth amongst men. In fact, during His triumphant entry into Jerusalem, He used a borrowed donkey, which indicates that He never even owned one. Romans 8:29-30 says, *"For whom he did foreknow, he also did predestinate to be conformed to the image of his Son, that he might be the firstborn among many brethren. Moreover whom he did predestinate, them he also called: and whom he called, them he also justified: and whom he justified, them he also glorified."* Also, Acts 3:13 says, *"The God of Abraham, and of Isaac, and of Jacob, the God of our fathers, hath glorified his Son Jesus; whom ye delivered up, and denied him in the presence of Pilate, when he was determined to let him go."*

Henceforth, almost everybody is seeking some sort of breakthrough and open doors in life, especially with regard to their finances, health, business, marriage, etc. This shows that we all need God's blessings, and we all want to benefit from the mercy and lovingkindness of God. However, have we ever asked ourselves, "How can God benefit from us?" The fact is, it is not wrong to seek breakthrough or God's benefits, but in seeking God's blessings or benefits, we must always keep the interests of God at heart if we truly want to be blessed by God, enjoy His benefits, and walk victoriously in life. For example, you cannot succeed as a good businessman or woman without keeping the interests of your partner or investor in mind. Every good businessman or woman who does business in partnership will always think of what's in it for his/her partner or what can his/her partner profit from the business in order to motivate him/her to invest more into it.

Biblically, as believers, we are considered as "children of God", but at the same time, God goes into partnership with us in order to accomplish His purpose right here on earth. Even marriage is a relationship that is based on a lifetime partnership agreement, which is why it is not to be taken lightly. Our divine partnership with God is based upon the Covenant Blood of our Lord Jesus Christ, as well as our faith. For instance, Abraham, "the father of faith", was not only a partner of God through faith, but he was a "friend of God", as well. This is because God benefited from Abraham's faith and obedience, especially when Abraham's faith was used to accomplish God's plans and purpose in the establishment of nations – 2 Chronicles 20:7, *"Art not thou our God, who didst drive out the inhabitants of this land before thy people Israel, and gavest it to the seed of Abraham thy friend for ever?"* Also see Isaiah 41:8.

If we, as believers, desire the blessings and benefits of God, we must begin by strengthening our partnership with God, through our faithfulness, obedience, and prayerfulness, as well as committing ourselves to consistent fasting and reading more of God's Word. With this, we will be able to ask ourselves, "What is in my life from which God can benefit?" This question will mean that you are having God's interests at heart and that you want a fair deal with Him.

Chapter Seven

The Walk of a New Man

As a matter of fact, once we become born-again, we automatically enter into a partnership agreement with God, and this partnership is designed to accomplish God's plans and purpose here on earth. However, often times, we don't seem to consider God's interests in this unique partnership deal, but we only think about our own selfish interests. This is why we always find ourselves wrestling with the will of God and struggling unnecessarily in life. For example, most often, we pray to God for breakthrough in different areas of our lives, but we have never asked ourselves, "What would God benefit from our breakthrough?" We want to get married, so we pray to God for favor to get married, but have we asked ourselves, "What would God benefit from our marriage?" Will God be glorified in our marriage or will God be disgraced in it, due to dishonesty, infidelity, early divorce, etc.? – (Genesis 2:24-25, Matthew 5:31-32, Matthew 19:1-11, 1 Corinthians 7:1-5, Hebrews 13:4, 1 Peter 3:1-7). We need children, so we pray to God for children, but have we asked ourselves, "What would God benefit from our children?" Do we pray for children so that when we have them, we will spoil them or corrupt their morals by allowing them the freedom to raise themselves, watch whatever they want on television, or allow them to go wherever they want because they are young adults? Are we going to allow our children to control us, as it is in our society today or are we going to control and discipline our children in the fear of the Lord, no matter what the state or government says? Are we going to allow our immoral society to corrupt the godly virtues of our children by making them prostitutes, drug addicts, gangsters, alcoholics, criminals, and murderers or are we going to dedicate our children to the Lord as Hannah did with Samuel? Are we going to instill Christian discipline and values in our children so that wherever they go, they will be obedient unto us, listen to us knowing that we have their best interests at heart, respect elders everywhere, and honor the Lord through the decent life they live? – (Exodus 20:12, Proverb 13:24, Proverb 19:18, Proverb 22:6, Proverb 29:17, Ephesians 6:1-4, Hebrews 12:5-10). We pray to God for healing because we are tired of being sick, but have we asked ourselves, "What would God benefit from our healing or recovery?" Do we pray for healing so that when we are healed, we will later forget where God took us from and go back to living selfishly, dishonestly, and immorally? Do we pray for healing so that when we are healed, God will be benefited, especially by helping others, doing good to all, laying down our lives for others, doing the right thing, and honoring God in our characters?

To all you "selfish and mean individuals", you are praying for God to restore your business or make it grow bigger, but what's in it for God? How can God benefit from that business of yours, when you are giving all the excuses and telling all the lies for not helping your fellow man? How can God benefit from your business when the maximum you give to the poor street beggar is far less than his daily bread? How can God benefit from you when you do not treat people as you would want others to treat you? The fact is, if your fellow man, whom you see, cannot benefit from you, how then can God, whom you cannot see, benefit from you? – 1 John 4:7-21, *"Beloved, let us love one another: for love is of God; and every one that loveth is born of God, and knoweth God. He that loveth not knoweth not God; for God is love. In this was manifested the love of God toward us, because that God sent his only begotten Son into the world, that we might live through him. Herein is love, not that we loved God, but that he loved us, and sent his Son to be the propitiation for our sins. Beloved, if God so loved us, we ought also to love one another. No man hath seen God at any time. If we love one another, God dwelleth in us, and his love is perfected in us. Hereby know we that we dwell in him, and he in us, because he hath given us of his Spirit. And we have seen and do testify that the Father sent the Son to be the Saviour of the world. Whosoever shall confess that Jesus is the Son of God, God dwelleth in him, and he in God. And we have known and believed the love that God hath to us. God is love; and he that dwelleth in love dwelleth in God, and God in him. Herein is our love made perfect, that we may have boldness in the day of judgment: because as he is, so are we in this world. There is no fear in love; but perfect love casteth out fear: because fear hath torment. He that feareth is not made perfect in love. We love him, because he first loved us. If a man say, I love God, and hateth his brother, he is a liar: for he that loveth not his brother whom he hath seen, how can he love God whom he hath not seen? And this commandment have we from him, That he who loveth God love his brother also."*

It is true that in life, we all desire the best, but do we also desire the same for other people? Do you try to see what God sees or feels, or are you only concerned about your own feelings and desires of your heart? Do you try to see people as God sees them, or do you see people based on what you see, hear, or think about them? Being a god is seeing the world and mankind through the eyes and mind of God. Being a god is to see things from God's perspective, and not ours. Being a god is to see things from Jack's perspective, and not from Bill's perspective. Unlike Bill, Jack demonstrated humility by appreciating and worshipping God with a heart of thanksgiving for affording him the privilege of sharing God's burden by making him a god to other people who were in need.

Generally, in life, it takes the spirit of pride, arrogance, and selfishness to display an attitude of ingratitude and think that you deserve the best because it is your birthright to have what has been given to you graciously. On the other hand, it takes a great deal of humility, meekness, and simplicity to display an attitude of gratitude to God and man.

Often times, we become desirous of God's divine touch or even crave to experience the visitation of God's Angels, failing to realize that we encounter God's divine touch everyday, and we also see His Angels all around us. Unfortunately, due to our secular mentality and carnality, we just don't feel or recognize this experience. In reality, when we become too secular-minded and flesh-conscious, we get disconnected spiritually and get out of touch with our source of power. Likewise, our greed, selfishness, self-centeredness, pride and arrogance, as well as our misconception and wrong judgment of people have intensely blinded our eyes and prevented us from recognizing the lowly and simplistic presence of "God's angels" in our lives. Maybe, if we can just open our eyes and hearts a little more, then we will begin to see beyond our greed, pride, arrogance, hypocrisy, judgmental behavior, selfishness, and egoism and realize that this wonderful world is not just about us, but other people also exist. Recognizing the existence of other people and fulfilling our divine duties toward them will no doubt make us gods to them, especially when we meet them at the point of their needs.

As a matter of fact, religion, if not understood, can be a very dangerous tool for causing division and conflict in our world.

The fact is, you can be a devoted religious figure and not have a relationship with the Almighty God. Therefore, what is important is not religion, but our relationship with the Almighty God and our fellow human beings. In other words, our love for the Almighty God and our fellow human beings defines our religion. This was exactly the kind of message that the Lord Jesus Christ taught His followers, but in a more simplistic and profound manner. In a nutshell, He taught that love for God and our fellow human beings constituted the entirety of God's commandments. The prophet Job, for example, understood the truth and became one of God's favorite – for he neither belonged to Judaism, Christianity, or Islam, yet he had a "trusting" and "faithful" relationship with the Almighty God. The fact is, Job's religion was the condition of his "heart" and the perfection of his heart was reflected in his character, utterances, and deeds.

However, it is important that we understand that religion is fundamentally designed to teach us some of the complexities of life and the profundity of the spiritual world, as well as guide us in our relationship with the Almighty God. Unfortunately, this simple truth has been misunderstood and abused, especially by those greedy and selfish ones who define religion based on their deceptive views, self-righteousness, egoism, and extremism – as a result of this, religion is now being used as a conduit to manipulate and exploit the faithful in the Name of the Holy God, as well as create conflict in our world, divide God's children, and set us against one another. In conclusion, religion is the totality of love for God and our fellow human beings, irrespective of color, age, sex, race, nationality, creed, or religion!

When asked about the "great" commandments in the Law, the Lord Jesus Christ got right to the point and told the tempter (the lawyer) that a complete and passionate love for God and our fellow men are the two "great" commandments on which the Law and prophets are based – Matthew 22:34-40, *"But when the Pharisees had heard that he had put the Sadducees to silence, they were gathered together. Then one of them, which was a lawyer, asked him a question, tempting him, and saying, Master, which is the great commandment in the law? Jesus said unto him, Thou shalt love the Lord thy God with all thy heart, and with all thy soul, and with all thy mind. This is the first and great commandment. And the second is like unto it, Thou shalt love thy neighbour as thyself. On these two commandments hang all the law and the prophets."*

The above Scripture teaches a very simple yet profound virtue and truth about life. For instance, loving the Almighty God with our entire being (spirit, heart, mind, and soul) simply means honoring and respecting God in our character, and enduring with God in all circumstances. It also means, communicating with God consistently, seeking the will of God in all things, abstaining from all appearances of evil, doing the right thing in the fear of the Lord, pleasing the Lord in all that we do, living righteously and faithfully, etc. Likewise, loving your neighbor as yourself means seeing other people as you see yourself and treating other people as you would like to be treated. Additionally, it also means sharing the pain, grief, and suffering of others, rejoicing with those who rejoice, seeing people as God sees them, stretching forth your hands to those who need your help, and if possible, be a god or Jesus to your generation.

Chapter Eight

Who Is Your Neighbor?

In simplifying the practicality of loving your neighbor as yourself, our Lord Jesus Christ passionately told the story of the Good Samaritan, but before going any further, it is important that we gain some general knowledge on the Samaritans in order to better understand the characteristics of the Good Samaritan. If you look closely, you will realize that the Lord Jesus Christ made many references to the Samaritans and even interacted with a few of them on and off the record. The question is, "What was so special about these people that attracted the Lord Jesus Christ to them?" Well, from the general point of view, most of the Samaritans were considered as "low-life" people, mainly because most of them worshipped idols and did not have much interest in religion and education, as compared to the Jews – See 2 Kings 17:29. In addition, most of the Samaritan women were domestic workers or prostitutes. For these reasons, the Jews looked down on them and had little or no respect for them. Ironically, most of the Samaritans are said to be of African descent, but there was something special about them that attracted the Lord Jesus Christ to their lives. They had the characteristics of being humble, simple-minded, giving, kindhearted, caring, lovers of strangers (hospitable), and very grateful.

Initially, when the Lord Jesus Christ commissioned His twelve disciples, He forbade them from entering into the cities of the Samaritans, due to their corrupted lives – See Matthew 10:5. Again, the prostitute whom the Lord Jesus Christ met at the well was also a Samaritan – See John 4:1-29.

Most of all, when the Lord Jesus Christ healed the Ten Lepers, it was the Samaritan amongst them who came back to the Lord Jesus Christ to say, "Thank-you" and gave glory to the Almighty God for his miracle (healing). Meanwhile, the remaining nine, who happened to all be Jews, walked away without expressing a word of gratitude – Luke 17:10-16, " *So likewise ye, when ye shall have done all those things which are commanded you, say, We are unprofitable servants: we have done that which was our duty to do. And it came to pass, as he went to Jerusalem, that he passed through the midst of Samaria and Galilee. And as he entered into a certain village, there met him ten men that were lepers, which stood afar off: And they lifted up their voices, and said, Jesus, Master, have mercy on us. And when he saw them, he said unto* them, Go shew yourselves unto the priests. And it came to pass, that, as they went, they were cleansed. And one of them, when he saw that he was healed, turned back, and with a loud voice glorified God, And fell down on his face at his feet, giving him thanks: and he was a Samaritan."

Regarding the story of the Good Samaritan, let us carefully read the below – Luke 10:25-37, "And, behold, a certain lawyer stood up, and tempted him, saying, Master, what shall I do to inherit eternal life? He said unto him, What is written in the law? how readest thou? And he answering said, Thou shalt love the Lord thy God with all thy heart, and with all thy soul, and with all thy strength, and with all thy mind; and thy neighbour as thyself. And he said unto him, Thou hast answered right: this do, and thou shalt live. But he, willing to justify himself, said unto Jesus, And who is my neighbour? And Jesus answering said, A certain man went down from Jerusalem to Jericho, and fell among thieves, which stripped him of his raiment, and wounded him, and departed, leaving him half dead. And by chance there came down a certain priest that way: and when he saw him, he passed by on the other side. And likewise a Levite, when he was at the place, came and looked on him, and passed by on the other side. But a certain Samaritan, as he journeyed, came where he was: and when he saw him, he had compassion on him, And went to him, and bound up his wounds, pouring in oil and wine, and set him on his own beast, and brought him to an inn, and took care of him. And on the morrow when he departed, he took out two pence, and gave them to the host, and said unto him, Take care of him; and whatsoever thou spendest more, when I come again, I will repay thee. Which now of these three, thinkest thou, was neighbour unto him that fell among the thieves? And he said, He that shewed mercy on him. Then said Jesus unto him, Go, and do thou likewise."

In the above Scripture, the Good Samaritan displayed the essence of love and defined a neighbor from God's perspective. For example, John 3:16 teaches us that love is incomplete in the absence of giving, which is why God gave His only Son to the world, in order to prove His love to mankind. Therefore, if we love somebody (whether it be our neighbor, etc.), we must prove our love by giving our time, service, finances, material resources, or even our lives. In the case of the Good Samaritan, he not only gave his finances, but gladly and humbly gave his time and services to the wounded man. He (the Good Samaritan) first of all rendered first aid unto the wounded man, next put him upon his own beast, then took him to an inn (in modern times, he put him into his car and drove him to a hotel). However, the above Scripture makes us to understand that prior to the arrival of the Good Samaritan, a priest (Bishop, Prophet, or Rev. Dr.) first came on the scene and saw the wounded man struggling for his life, but did nothing. Probably, he said to himself, "Who knows, maybe he stole from somebody and was beaten up for it. Well, the Bible says we must be wise, so let me mind my own business." Second, a Levite (Pastor or Man of God) arrived on the scene and saw the pitiful condition of this wounded man, but only looked on and did nothing. I'm sure he may have said to himself, "Maybe this guy doesn't go to church, which is why God allowed those thieves to beat him up like that or maybe because he doesn't pay his tithes."

We must remember that our attitude of being judgmental in most cases prevents us from obeying the Holy Spirit, walking in the will of God, and doing good. This is why the Lord Jesus Christ warned us against judging others – Matthew 7:1, ***"Judge not, that ye be not judged."*** Moreover, Luke 10:25-37 makes us to understand that the Good Samaritan was an ordinary man who was neither a pastor nor a bishop, but he responded to the call of God in humility by allowing himself to be used as a "god" to a man he did not know from anywhere. In this regard, we must understand that it takes humility and obedience to demonstrate God's love practically to a fellow human being by giving your service, time, financial resources, etc. Contrariwise, it takes pride, arrogance, disobedience, and a judgmental spirit to turn your eyes and ignore the needs of a fellow human being.

Meanwhile, it is important to acknowledge in this context that the Good Samaritan did not share a fence or wall with the wounded man, yet he saw him as his neighbor and showed him love. The Good Samaritan and the wounded man were not next-door neighbors nor did they live in the same neighborhood, community, or area, yet the Good Samaritan saw the wounded man as his neighbor, proving to him that love is stronger than our pride, arrogance, and judgmental spirit and shines even brighter than our eyesight. The Good Samaritan also proved beyond all reasonable doubt that love can shorten any distance, and it knows no boundary, color, tribe, religion, nationality, or creed. The Good Samaritan became a god to the wounded man when he met him at the point of his needs. This shows that in life, whenever you meet people at the point of their needs, you practically become a god to them because they will never forget you, even if it was for the glass of water you gave them when they were dying of thirst.

Dearly beloved, your neighbor is that brother or sister next door, as well as that brother or sister across the ocean who is standing in need on the other side of the world. Your neighbor is that hungry-looking, pale, and emaciated stranger who came asking you for help, but you told him that you didn't have it, when in fact you did. Your neighbor is that poor, broke, and sickly-looking man who tried to intercept you along the way, but you pretended as if he didn't exist, by turning your face on the other side and walking passed him, just as the Priest and Levite did to the wounded man. Your neighbor is that young man or woman across the street who is not in school because his or her parents cannot afford school fees. Your neighbor is that sorrowful, young prostitute who is selling her precious body to survive, about whom you have always gossiped, but have never cared to know her pain and struggles. Your neighbor is that drug addict or alcoholic of whom you have always avoided and made mockery, but have never made any effort to know the story of his/her life. Your neighbor is that dirty street kid whom you always condemn, but never took the time to talk to him/her about his/her problem. Only if we can stop being judgmental and put a little love in our hearts, then the great sacrifice of our Lord Jesus Christ will never be in vain. The Almighty God has made us gods on many occasions, but we have refused to honor Him in our divine responsibilities, due to our pride, greed, arrogance, selfishness, egocentricity, and self-righteousness.

Unfortunately, as a preacher of truth, I have no idea of what man has turned this wonderful world into. For example, on Wall Street, business executives are negotiating millions of dollars in profit for their businesses or corporations, but on the streets of the Bronx and Brooklyn, thousands of people in those areas go to bed hungry every night and some even sleep on the streets. It's all about the simple message of loving your neighbor as yourself. In Washington, D.C., politicians and Congressmen/women discuss a national budget that amounts to billions of dollars, while in their backyard in East Washington and in front of the Capitol building, hundreds of people sleep on the streets at night, and thousands are starving everyday. It is all due to the neglect of the simple message of loving your neighbor as yourself. In Hollywood, you have movie stars spending millions of dollars recklessly and extravagantly on houses, cars, and other irrelevant material things, but when they die, they will leave them with people who did not even work for them, while hundreds of thousands of people sleep on the streets and in huts across the oceans, in Africa, Asia, South America, and even right here in the United States. It's all about the neglect of the simple message of loving your neighbor as yourself. What then can you say to me about the world in which we live?

Frustrated by the deception and hypocrisy of most so-called "Christians", I tearfully wrote the below poem, ***"Prisoner of Faith"***:

I've endeavored to live a life
contrary to the norms of the society.
Challenged by my passionate desire
and ego to reject the world,
I still found it difficult to
surrender my will completely
to the power of Heaven.

Shackled in my belief,
I consciously choose to live abnormally
in a world where everything seems normal,
especially lies, discrimination, fornication,
idolatry, sexual sins, deception,
swindling others, etc.

Choosing to live righteously

*was the beginning of my struggle
and worldly sorrow,
especially when I saw no gain in my pain,
yet I refused to be subjected
to the attractions, pleasures, and
cares of this world.*

*O how difficult it is to maintain
one's focus in the midst of scorn,
ridicule, temptation, and desperation.
Yes, I'm a prisoner of my faith,
a redeemed prisoner, destined to
walk in the Light of Truth,
just to set the captives free.*

*Questing the mystery of life,
and delving the causation of nature,
still I found no answers in science
and human philosophies.
In the midst of my grief and frustration,
I went beyond my human capacity
and earned more degrees,
just to find logic in faith
and reason in creation.
Unfortunately, my achievements
became foolishness, and my life
became filled with sorrow and confusion.*

*Traveling the world over
and practicing the science of ancient mysticism
and occultism, still I became more
confused and very empty.*

*Wandering aimlessly from one religion
to another, questing to find solace,
enlightenment, peace, and happiness,
still I became the victim of hypnotization,*

exploitation, and manipulation.

*The simple truth became a complicated lie,
and the preachers became propagators
of deception, through their messages
of manipulation and prosperity.
Performing satanic miracles
and preaching the doom message of the End Time,
they quickly allured huge followers,
only to be used in building their empire.*

*Instead of preaching and demonstrating love,
which should be the foundation and essence of their faith,
they boldly and shamelessly exploit and
manipulate the poor and ignorant,
in the name of the very God whom
they have put a price tag on,
amassing huge wealth at the
ignorant expense of the faithful.*

*Seeing all of these deceptions and evils,
I'm not deterred; rather, I remain
a prisoner of my faith, not walking
in the path of man or seeking vain glory
and perishable vanities, but walking
in the path of light, in the humility
of the Holy Spirit, and in the
simplicity of the Lord Jesus Christ.*

*Truly, I'm a prisoner of my faith,
a redeemed prisoner, who is determined
to walk in the Light of Truth, only to
set the captives free.
I'm not a Christian, but a lover and
faithful follower of the Lord Jesus Christ,
because religion divides and fuels hate.*

Chapter Nine

The True Giver

Before turning the coin on the other side, it is important that we come to understand the characteristics of the three kinds of givers we have in our world today. The three kinds of givers we have in our world today are the Impressive Giver, the Selfish or Egocentric Giver, and the Silent Giver.

The **Impressive Givers** are those who give to impress others, but such giving is really not from the heart; rather, it is done to boast or show off. This category of giver is the one who gives so that others will see them as being kind and good when in reality, they are not. These people are in fact hypocrites who are no better than the politicians who give to be seen and praised by men in order to win the support of the "ignorant masses". Unfortunately, these people give "politically", and not from the heart, because if a person is in need of help or assistance that will benefit his/her life, the impressive giver will never give that person the help or assistance of which he/she stands in need.

The **Selfish or Egocentric Givers** are those arrogant and egocentric givers who give only if they are going to be benefited in some way from the person(s) to whom they are giving or the place where they are giving. This category of giver is no better than the business people who give only if their giving is an "indirect investment" into themselves, but the truth is, their giving is not from the heart. Actually, these people are very insensitive to the needs of others because their giving is based on profit (what they will get in return). These people are simply greedy, selfish, egocentric, and very secular-minded. In most cases, when these selfish givers are giving, they always want to know the background of the person to whom they are giving or the root of their problems. They use this as an alibi in order to suppress or ignore their divine nature of giving, and at the end of the day, they just wouldn't give a dime. The fact of the matter is, if the Good Samaritan would have investigated the background or causation of the Wounded Man's problem, he wouldn't have been "the Good Samaritan" because the Wounded Man would have died in the process, even before concluding his investigation.

The truth is, anyone who makes up or comes up with an excuse for not doing good to his/her fellow human being is simply not a good person. This is because a good person perceives no excuse for not doing good. For example, the Good Samaritan perceived no excuse for not helping the Wounded Man. In fact, if the Good Samaritan had wanted to use an excuse for not helping the Wounded Man, he would have used all the excuses in the world, especially since the Wounded Man was a stranger he did not know from anywhere. Besides that, the condition in which he met the Wounded Man was enough of an excuse for not helping him. He met a man who was beaten up and almost naked, who may have been a criminal who was being victimized by his fellow criminals or the people from whom he tried to steal. However, having been pure-minded and kindhearted, the Good Samaritan saw the Wounded Man as a human being in need of help, which suggests that if we accept people as they present themselves, as we see them, or as God would see them, we will definitely find no excuse for not doing good to our fellow human beings.

The **Silent Givers** are those divine givers who give in secret and expect to receive nothing in return. These people give because they are not only sensitive to the needs of others, but they always try to put themselves in the shoes of others. In a nutshell, the silent givers give in obedience to God's Word and not for benefit, show, boast, or name.

Notwithstanding, contrary to the characteristics of the Good Samaritan, the Lord Jesus Christ told the story of the Rich Man (Dives), and the Poor Beggar (Lazarus) – Luke 16:19-31, "*There was a certain rich man, which was clothed in purple and fine linen, and fared sumptuously every day: And there was a certain beggar named Lazarus, which was laid at his gate, full of sores, And desiring to be fed with the crumbs which fell from the rich man's table: moreover the dogs came and licked his sores. And it came to pass, that the beggar died, and was carried by the angels into Abraham's bosom: the rich man also died, and was buried; And in hell he lift up his eyes, being in torments, and seeth Abraham afar off, and Lazarus in his bosom. And he cried and said, Father Abraham, have mercy on me, and send Lazarus, that he may dip the tip of his finger in water, and cool my tongue; for I am tormented in this flame. But Abraham said, Son, remember that thou in thy lifetime receivedst thy good things, and likewise Lazarus evil things: but now he is comforted, and thou art tormented. And beside all this, between us and you there is a great gulf fixed: so that they which would pass from hence to you cannot; neither can they pass to us, that would come from thence. Then he said, I pray thee therefore, father, that thou wouldest send him to my father's house: For I have five brethren; that he may testify unto them, lest they also come into this place of torment. Abraham saith unto him, They have Moses and the prophets; let them hear them. And he said, Nay, father Abraham: but if one went unto them from the dead, they will repent. And he said unto him, If they hear not Moses and the prophets, neither will they be persuaded, though one rose from the dead."*

According to the above Scripture, God graciously afforded the rich man (Dives) the opportunity and privilege to be a blessing and a god to Lazarus, the beggar, but because of his greed, pride, arrogance, selfishness, materialism, and egocentricity, he categorically refused to allow himself to be a "god" and a blessing to poor Lazarus. When he died, he left behind all his precious wealth and riches and went directly to hell-fire. The fact is, the rich man (Dives) did not go to hell-fire because of his wealth or riches, No! He went to hell-fire because God did not benefit from his wealth and riches. Dives, the rich man, went to hell-fire because when he was on earth, he enjoyed in surplus and comfort, while the dogs licked the sores of poor Lazarus at his gate. Dives, the rich man, went to hell-fire because love was absent from his heart. He allowed the spirit of pride, arrogance, materialism, and egocentricity to blind him so intensely that he refused to see the hungry, suffering, and dying presence of Lazarus at his gate. Dives, the rich man, went to hell-fire because in his pride and arrogance, Lazarus, the beggar, was too insignificant for him to even talk to. Dives, the rich man, went to hell-fire because in his pride, arrogance, and egocentricity, the leftover crumbs from his "royal" table were too expensive and valuable for "insignificant" and "dirty" Lazarus to eat. Dives, the rich man, went to hell-fire because in his greed and selfishness, he thought that the world revolved around him and that nobody else mattered. Dives, the rich man, went to hell-fire because he committed a great sin by being insensitive to the needs of Lazarus and not loving his neighbor as himself.

Biblically, nobody goes to hell-fire because he or she is rich, and nobody goes to Heaven because he or she is poor, No! Scriptures make it clear that sinners are the people who go to hell-fire, while the righteous are the ones who go to Heaven. Hence, Dives, the rich man, went to hell-fire because of his insensitivity in addressing the needs of his neighbor, Lazarus when he was in the position to do so. This attitude no doubt made him a sinner. On the other hand, Lazarus, the poor beggar, went to Heaven, not because of his poverty, but because he was a righteous man, in spite of his poverty.

In Matthew 25:31-46, our Lord Jesus Christ spoke of the eternal consequence for those who allowed the spirit of pride, arrogance, greed, selfishness, and egocentricity to prevent them from loving their neighbors as themselves and meeting them at the point of their needs – "*When the Son of man shall come in his glory, and all the holy angels with him, then shall he sit upon the throne of his glory: And before him shall be gathered all nations: and he shall separate them one from another, as a shepherd divideth his sheep from the goats: And he shall set the sheep on his right hand, but the goats on the left. Then shall the King say unto them on his right hand, Come, ye blessed of my Father, inherit the kingdom prepared for you from the foundation of the world: For I was an hungred, and ye gave me meat: I was thirsty, and ye gave me drink: I was a stranger, and ye took me in: Naked, and ye clothed me: I was sick, and ye visited me: I was in prison, and ye came unto me. Then shall the righteous answer him, saying, Lord, when saw we thee an hungred, and fed thee? or thirsty, and gave thee drink? When saw we thee a stranger, and took thee in? or naked, and clothed thee? Or when saw we thee sick, or in prison, and came unto thee? And the King shall answer and say unto them, Verily I say unto you, Inasmuch as ye have done it unto one of the least of these my brethren, ye have done it unto me. Then shall he say also unto them on the left hand, Depart from me, ye cursed, into everlasting fire, prepared for the devil and his angels: For I was an hungred, and ye gave me no meat: I was thirsty, and ye gave me no drink: I was a stranger, and ye took me not in: naked, and ye clothed me not: sick, and in prison, and ye visited me not. Then shall they also answer him, saying, Lord, when saw we thee an hungred, or athirst, or a stranger, or naked, or sick, or in prison, and did not minister unto thee? Then shall he answer them, saying, Verily I say unto you, Inasmuch as ye did it not to one of the least of these, ye did it not to me. And these shall go away into everlasting punishment: but the righteous into life eternal."*

In this Scripture, our Lord Jesus Christ made it clear that when He shall return to judge the human race, He shall sit upon His Throne and separate the sheep from the goat. This means that He shall put those in the "Sheep Department" on the right-hand side and those in the "Goat Department" on the left-hand side. Referring to Himself as the King (the Judge of the World), the Lord Jesus Christ will bless those in the Sheep Department (His right-hand side) and promises that He will share His glorious kingdom with them, because when He was hungry, they gave Him food to eat, and when He was thirsty, they gave Him drink. He even went further to say that when He was a stranger, they took Him in; when He was naked, they clothed Him; when He was sick, they visited Him; and when He was in prison, they came and ministered unto Him. The righteous (those in the Sheep Department) will then be amazed and ask the Lord Jesus Christ, "When did we see you in any of the above circumstances and attended unto you?" The Master will then smile and say to them, "Because you had done it to one of the 'least' of these, my brethren, you had done it to me."

The Master, Jesus Christ, will then turn to those at His left-hand side (the Goat Department) and tell them to depart from Him because their pride, arrogance, greed, selfishness, and egocentricity have brought an eternal curse and damnation upon them; therefore, they are condemned into the everlasting fire that has been prepared for Satan (the devil) and his angels. This is because when He was hungry, they did not give Him food; when He was thirsty, they did not give Him drink; when He was a stranger, they did not take Him in or welcome Him into their homes; when He was naked, they did not give Him clothes to wear; when He was sick, they did not visit Him; and when He was in prison, they did not minister unto Him. Those in the Goat Department or on the left-hand side shall then argue their case and say, "Lord, when did we ever see you in any of the above circumstances or in conditions of need?" The Lord Jesus Christ shall then remind them of His lowly visitation in the appearance of the ordinary people we see around us everyday and tell them that because they did not do these things for the "least" of these (the ordinary people they see everyday), they did not do it to Him. Therefore, they will be cast into everlasting punishment, while the righteous will have life eternal.

The simple, but very significant message in the above tells us that in this life, whatever we do for our fellow man (regardless of whom the person is), we do it to the Lord Jesus Christ and His Father. This also gives us the understanding that every human being in the world represents the physical presence of the Lord Jesus Christ here on earth, as long as that person is created in the image and likeness of the Most High God, especially those who are our fellow believers.

Sadly, there are millions of people in our world today who have been terribly wounded one way or the other by the "thief of life" – the devil (John 10:10). These people have been wounded spiritually, mentally, emotionally, morally, economically, socially, and even physically, just as the Wounded Man whom the Good Samaritan rescued. Unfortunately, most of these wounded people in life have not been opportune to come in contact with the "Good Samaritan", so as a result, they are living their lives hopelessly and painfully on the edge, having no idea of what God has in store for them in the future.

Likewise, there are thousands of homeless in our world who have been economically, morally, and socially wounded, and they just need that "Good Samaritan" to cross their path and demonstrate to them in love that there is hope for the hopeless and a way out of their situation and that all is not lost. Also, there are thousands of young men and women out there on our streets living their lives in the midst of confusion, rejection, bitterness, unforgiveness, low self-esteem, disappointment, abuse, injustice, discrimination, and violence who are just prostituting, dealing drugs, abusing alcohol, etc. They have been badly wounded spiritually, mentally, morally, and socially and just need a "Good Samaritan" to demonstrate to them in love that there is a better way and that life is not always unfair. In addition, there are hundreds of relationships and marriages in our world that have been wounded, but without the intervention of that "Good Samaritan", those relationships and marriages will be destroyed, and children born out of those relationships and marriages will be even more wounded than their parents. Today, you can be that "Good Samaritan" about whom the Lord Jesus Christ was talking. If you can just put a little love in your heart, you will surely make the difference.

Hundreds of single mothers in our cities have been badly wounded, some of whom have even turned to drug addiction and prostitution, while others are about to commit suicide, due to the pain and frustration of life, just because that "Good Samaritan" has not yet rescued them to take them to the "Inn of Life".

Brothers and sisters, what are you doing in the fullness of your God-given conscious? Believe it or not, you are that "Good Samaritan" whom God has prepared for this moment, but because you have refused to listen to the voice of the Holy Spirit in obedience, you are now behaving like Dives, the Rich Man.

The fact is, we often see people on the streets and assume that they have their acts together and that all is well with them, not knowing that underneath that facade is someone who has been badly wounded. In our world today, people are so concerned about themselves and their own issues that they are too blind to see those who are badly wounded and in need of our help. We must stop being judgmental and self-righteous and begin to demonstrate the true meaning of love if we are to be the "god" whom God intended us to be.

In his work, "What Do We Do With This, Jesus?" Douglas Kaine McKelvey expressed the profundity of Jesus' teachings when he wrote, "...He thought that the least were the greatest, the rejected were the blessed, the wise were the foolish, the weak were the strong, and the secure were the lost. He taught that people should selflessly love, not just their friends and families – which would have been difficult enough – but strangers and enemies as well. He called on those possessed by their possessions to leave their wealth behind, to follow Him into a life of uncertain suffering for the one promised consolation of His love. His words grew so appalling one afternoon that many of His followers gave it up for good and returned home, muttering that His teaching was too hard. They had had enough. Those who stayed were apparently in too deep already. Most scandalous of all was the way Jesus publicly and persistently rejected the proud, self-righteous religious leaders of the day and instead drew prostitutes, half-breeds, political revolutionaries, smelly fishermen, and turncoat tax-collectors into His circle of friends – all of whom soon and somehow found themselves, by His very acceptance, transformed from what they had always thought they were into a new existence as children of God."

Additionally, when Saul (prior to his conversion and to him becoming "Paul") was on his way to persecute the disciples of the Lord Jesus Christ in Damascus, the Lord Jesus Christ intercepted his evil mission and arrested him in the brightness of a light from Heaven and said to him, "Saul, Saul, why persecutes thou me?" In other words, He said, "Saul, Saul why are you persecuting me?" Notice that the Lord Jesus Christ did not say, "Saul, Saul, why persecutes thou my people?" or "Saul, Saul, why are you persecuting my people?" This clearly indicates that touching a child of God is no doubt touching the Lord Jesus Christ Himself. Likewise, doing good to a child of God or anybody for that matter, is no doubt doing it to the Lord Jesus Christ Himself – Acts 9:1-6, *"And Saul, yet breathing out threatenings and slaughter against the disciples of the Lord, went unto the high priest, And desired of him letters to Damascus to the synagogues, that if he found any of this way, whether they were men or women, he might bring them bound unto Jerusalem. And as he journeyed, he came near Damascus: and suddenly there shined round about him a light from heaven: And he fell to the earth, and heard a voice saying unto him, Saul, Saul, why persecutest thou me? And he said, Who art thou, Lord? And the Lord said, I am Jesus whom thou persecutest: it is hard for thee to kick against the pricks. And he trembling and astonished said, Lord, what wilt thou have me to do? And the Lord said unto him, Arise, and go into the city, and it shall be told thee what thou must do."*

However, understanding the above Scripture from the Christian point of view, the Lord Jesus Christ warned of how we should treat one another, especially as believers – Matthew 18:4-6, *"Whosoever therefore shall humble himself as this little child, the same is greatest in the kingdom of heaven. And whoso shall receive one such little child in my name receiveth me. But whoso shall offend one of these little ones which believe in me, it were better for him that a millstone were hanged about his neck, and that he were drowned in the depth of the sea."* Likewise, the Apostle Paul, being in subjection to the teachings of the Lord Jesus Christ, wrote to the Galatians and urged them to do good to all men, especially unto fellow believers – Galatians 6:9-10, *"And let us not be weary in well doing: for in due season we shall reap, if we faint not. As we have therefore opportunity, let us do good unto all men, especially unto them who are of the household of faith."* This Scripture teaches that whatever good a man does to another man is never in vain because someday when he least expects it, he shall reap whatever good he did. The fact is, there is no such thing as infertile or barren ground when sowing a good seed, meaning that every good seed that is sown into the life of somebody bears good fruit one way or the other.

Also, 2 Corinthians 9:6-10 says, *"But this I say, He which soweth sparingly shall reap also sparingly; and he which soweth bountifully shall reap also bountifully. Every man according as he purposeth in his heart, so let him give; not grudgingly, or of necessity: for God loveth a cheerful giver. And God is able to make all grace abound toward you; that ye, always having all sufficiency in all things, may abound to every good work: (As it is written, He hath dispersed abroad; he hath given to the poor: his righteousness remaineth for ever. Now he that ministereth seed to the sower both minister bread for your food, and multiply your seed sown, and increase the fruits of your righteousness;)."*

This Scripture teaches that our act of giving must be from the heart and must be done with the freedom of God within us, or else we will not receive the blessing that we so desire. It also teaches that when we are giving to others, we must always give our best, and not our worst. For example, if we are giving out clothes, we should give out clothes that we ourselves would wear, or if it is some other usable item, it must be something that we ourselves would use. If we are giving out money, we should give it in such a way that it would benefit the person to whom we are giving it, especially depending upon what we have in our possession. Additionally, Proverbs 3:27-28 teaches that if it is within our power to do good to anyone who is in need, we should not hesitate to do good to that person – *"Withhold not good from them to whom it is due, when it is in the power of thine hand to do it. Say not unto thy neighbor, Go, and come again, and to morrow I will give; when thou hast it by thee."*

We must therefore be conscious of the fact that all that is within the earth belongs to the Most High God, including our wealth or the little dime in our pockets – Psalm 24:1, *"THE earth is the Lord's, and the fullness thereof; the world, and they that dwell therein."* This means, there is nothing that we have that can be withheld from the Almighty God. This is why King Solomon wrote in Proverbs 3:9-10, *"Honour the LORD with thy substance, and with the firstfruits of all thine increase: So shall thy barns be filled with plenty, and thy presses shall burst out with new wine."* This Scripture urges us to honor the Lord with our substance (wealth and riches), as well as to be faithful in paying our tithes (our first fruit or income), which is one-tenth or ten percent of our income or first fruits. However, the best way that we can honor God with our resources is to humbly invest in the lives of God's people (whether it be pastor, bishop, homeless, street people, prostitutes, addicts, or your needy next-door neighbor, etc.) and also to support anything that will glorify God.

Chapter Ten

Tithing, The Church, and The Contradiction

*C*oncerning the issue of tithing, Malachi 3:8-12 says, *"Will a man rob God? Yet ye have robbed me. But ye say, Wherein have we robbed thee? In tithes and offerings. Ye are cursed with a curse: for ye have robbed me, even this whole nation. Bring ye all the tithes into the storehouse, that there may be meat in mine house, and prove me now herewith, saith the Lord of hosts, if I will not open you the windows of heaven, and pour you out a blessing, that there shall not be room enough to receive it. And I will rebuke the devourer for your sakes, and he shall not destroy the fruits of your ground; neither shall your vine cast her fruit before the time in the field, saith the LORD of hosts. And all nations shall call you blessed: for ye shall be a delightsome land, saith the LORD of hosts ".* This Scripture emphasizes the importance of paying our tithes, but we must pay close attention to the instructions and process.

There are two sides to the above Scripture. Unfortunately, most pastors only look at one side of the above Scripture and neglect the other side, probably because it does not reflect their interests or benefit them. The fact is, the above Scripture does not in anyway exempt pastors from paying their tithes, as long as they are on salary or doing some sort of business. Besides that, the tithing laws require that the priest (pastors, bishops, etc.) divide the tithes into several parts, giving the first portion to the poor, the widows, orphans, fatherless, etc., the second portion to the faithful Levites (the struggling but faithful evangelists and church workers, who are not on salary or are on a fixed income), and the third portion goes to the priest (the pastor or overseer) – Deuteronomy 14:22-29, *"Thou shalt truly tithe all the increase of thy seed, that the field bringeth forth year by year. And thou shalt eat before the LORD thy God, in the place which he shall choose to place his name there, the tithe of thy corn, of thy wine, and of thine oil, and the firstlings of thy herds and of thy flocks; that thou mayest learn to fear the LORD thy God always. And if the way be too long for thee, so that thou art not able to carry it; or if the place be too far from thee, which the LORD thy God shall choose to set his name there, when the LORD thy God hath blessed thee: Then shalt thou turn it into money, and bind up the money into thine hand, and shalt go unto the place which the LORD thy God shall choose: And thou shalt bestow that money for whatsoever thy soul lusteth after, for oxen, or for sheep, or for wine, or for strong drink, or for whatsoever thy* soul desireth: and thou shalt eat there before the LORD thy God, and thou shalt rejoice, thou, and thine household, **And the Levite that is within thy gates; thou shalt not forsake him: for he hath no part nor inheritance with thee. At the end of three years thou shalt bring forth all the tithe of thine increase the same year, and shalt lay it up within thy gates: And the Levite (because he hath no part nor inheritance with thee,) and the stranger, and the fatherless, and the widow, which are within thy gates, shall come, and shall eat and be satisfied; that the LORD thy God may bless thee in all the work of thine hand which thou doest. "**

The above Scripture clearly instructs us on how portions of the tithes should be used for the Levites (evangelists, church workers, etc.), the strangers, the widows, the fatherless, homeless, etc., making sure that they are satisfied with what they have been given, based upon what has been received as tithes. Also, Deuteronomy 26:12-13 says, "**When thou hast made an end of tithing all the tithes of thine increase the third year, which is the year of tithing, and hast given it unto the Levite, the stranger, the fatherless, and the widow, that they may eat within thy gates, and be filled; Then thou shalt say before the LORD thy God, I have brought away the hallowed things out of mine house, and also have given them unto the Levite, and unto the stranger, to the fatherless, and to the widow, according to all thy commandments which thou hast commanded me: I have not transgressed thy commandments, neither have I forgotten them.**"

In this regard, it is important to understand that the payment of our tithes is dependent upon our monthly, bi-weekly, or weekly income, or whatever we receive from the daily sales of our businesses. In the Old Testament time, the tithes were brought into the House of God during the Harvest, which can be related in this modern time as our "payday". We must therefore note that tithing is completely different from the regular "offering" we collect in the church. In fact, what they call "offering" is really not; rather, it is a "collection". An "offering" is related to sacrifice; in fact, in the Old Testament time, it was given to God in the form of animals, money, gold, etc., specifically when a person wanted God to do something for him or her or when God had already done something in the life of that person. Offerings were also given for atonement – See Exodus 30:9-20, Exodus 20:24, Exodus 35:5-29, Leviticus 1:2-17, Numbers 6:14-18, Deuteronomy 12:6-27, 1 Kings 3:4-15, Joel 1:9-13, Hebrews 10:5-18, etc.

However, "collection" is the weekly financial contribution gathered on the first day of the week (Sunday) for the running and development of the church. This was first initiated by the prophet Moses, and it continues in the New Testament times – 2 Chronicles 24:9, *"And they made a proclamation through Judah and Jerusalem, to bring in the LORD the **collection** that Moses the servant of God laid upon Israel in the wilderness."* Also, 1 Corinthians 16:1-2 says, *"NOW concerning the **collection** for the saints, as I have given order to the churches of Galatia, even so do ye. Upon the first day of the week let every one of you lay by him in store, as God hath prospered him, that there be no gatherings when I come."*

In order to better understand the act of robbing God in our possessions or in tithes and offerings, let me refer you to a practical Biblical example as it relates to the above. The New Testament tells us of a lovely couple (believers) who attempted to rob God out of their own wealth but were not that lucky to survive to tell the story – Acts 5:1-11, *"BUT a certain man named Ananias, with Sapphira his wife, sold a possession, And kept back part of the price, his wife also being privy to it, and brought a certain part, and laid it at the apostles' feet. But Peter said, Ananias, why hath Satan filled thine heart to lie to the Holy Ghost, and to keep back part of the price of the land? Whiles it remained, was it not thine own? and after it was sold, was it not thine own power? why hast thou conceived this thing in thine heart? Thou hast not lied unto men, but unto God. And Ananias hearing these words fell down, and gave up the ghost: and great fear came on all them that heard these things. And the young men arose, wound him up, and carried him out, and buried him. And it was about the space of three hours after, when his wife, not knowing what was done, came in. And Peter answered unto her, Tell me whether ye sold the land for so much? And she said, Yea, for so much. Then Peter said unto her, How is it that ye have agreed together to tempt the Spirit of the Lord? Behold, the feet of them which have buried thy husband are at the door ,and shall carry thee out. Then fell she down straightway at his feet, and yielded up the ghost: and the young men came in, and found her dead, and, carrying her forth, buried her by her husband. And great fear came upon all the church, and upon as many as heard these things."*

The above Scripture reveals the mysterious power of the Holy Spirit, indicating that nothing can be hidden from God. The selfishness and deception of Ananias and Sapphira can still be seen in our churches and in society today. The land they sold belonged to them, and they had the power to do whatever they wanted to do with the money. It is believed that they had earlier promised the church that when their land was sold, they would donate "all" of the money to the church. However, when the land was sold and they saw that the money was too much to giveaway to the work of God, they conspired to steal from it and only give a small portion to the church. They made a grave mistake because God never sleeps, and He takes all our promises regarding His business very seriously. Today, many people rob God and lie about it, thinking that they can get away with it. Nowadays, God's Holy Spirit does the striking more in the spiritual than in the physical. We must therefore be careful not to rob God and lie about it.

Ananias and his wife Sapphira were struck down by the Holy Spirit, not only because they lied to the Holy Spirit, but mainly because they robbed God and tried to cover it up with lies and deception.

The story of the Good Samaritan is the most realistic story of practical benevolence in the Holy Bible, which profoundly expresses the essence of loving your neighbors as yourself. It also demonstrates how the Almighty God, in the beauty of His power and glory, can make us gods to other people without even realizing it, especially by bringing us into physical contact with them at the point of their needs. God has graciously made some of us gods unknowingly in our offices, in our schools, in our workplaces, on our streets, in our communities, in our neighborhoods, in our cities, in our towns, in our villages, in our churches, and even in our very own homes. Unfortunately, our pride, arrogance, self-righteousness, egocentricity, disobedience, faithlessness, and ignorance have caused us to sin greatly against God. This attitude of ours has also caused us to miss out on the glorious and wondrous blessings that await those who respond with humility to the call of being gods to their fellow human beings, by meeting them at the point of their needs.

For example, even in the midst of his difficulties during his spiritual reconstruction process, David, the servant of God, was made a "god" to King Saul (his enemy) and with a great sense of humility and meekness of heart, he responded positively to the noble and honorable call of a god. This tells us that the Almighty God can make us gods to people in all circumstances, whether in our good times or in our bad times. The Most High God can also make us gods to our enemies, especially when we humble ourselves by opening our hearts with meekness and God's love.

David became a god to King Saul at the time when the Almighty God delivered the life of King Saul into the hands of David on two occasions. During those two occasions, David could have killed his number one enemy (King Saul) and become the King of Israel; however, he didn't do it because as a "god", David was only concerned about pleasing the Most High God and doing His will, and not his own. David's actions were positive, and they were in conformity to the will of God – 1 Samuel 24:1-15, *"And it came to pass, when Saul was returned from following the Philistines, that it was told him, saying, Behold, David is in the wilderness of Engedi. Then Saul took three thousand chosen men out of all Israel, and went to seek David and his men upon the rocks of the wild goats. And he came to the sheepcotes by the way, where was a cave; and Saul went in to cover his feet: and David and his men remained in the sides of the cave. And the men of David said unto him, Behold the day of which the Lord said unto thee, Behold, I will deliver thine enemy into thine hand, that thou mayest do to him as it shall seem good unto thee. Then David arose, and cut off the skirt of Saul's robe privily. And it came to pass afterward, that David's heart smote him, because he had cut off Saul's skirt. And he said unto his men, The Lord forbid that I should do this thing unto my master, the Lord's anointed, to stretch forth mine hand against him, seeing he is the anointed of the Lord. So David stayed his servants with* these words, and suffered them not to rise against Saul. But Saul rose up out of the cave, and went on his way. David also arose afterward, and went out of the cave, and cried after Saul, saying, My lord the king. And when Saul looked behind him, David stooped with his face to the earth, and bowed himself. And David said to Saul, Wherefore hearest thou men's words, saying, Behold, David seeketh thy hurt? Behold, this day thine eyes have seen how that the Lord had delivered thee to day into mine hand in the cave: and some bade me kill thee: but mine eye spared thee; and I said, I will not put forth mine hand against my lord; for he is the Lord's anointed. Moreover, my father, see, yea, see the skirt of thy robe in my hand: for in that I cut off the skirt of thy robe, and killed thee not, know thou and see that there is neither evil nor transgression in mine hand, and I have not sinned against thee; yet thou huntest my soul to take it. The Lord judge between me and thee, and the Lord avenge me of thee: but mine hand shall not be upon thee. As saith the proverb of the ancients, Wickedness proceedeth from the wicked: but mine hand shall not be upon thee. After whom is the king of Israel come out? after whom dost thou pursue? after a dead dog, after a flea. The Lord therefore be judge, and judge between me and thee, and see, and plead my cause, and deliver me out of thine hand." Also, see 1 Samuel 26:4-23.

In reality, when someone, especially your enemy, is given the opportunity to destroy your life (God forbid it), but instead, spares your life, then that person will automatically become a god to you. This is exactly how it was in the case of David and King Saul. After David spared the life of King Saul, his destiny was predicted from Saul's own mouth. King Saul even admitted that God was truly with David, and that he (David) certainly would become the next King of Israel. King Saul went on to confess that David was more righteous than he and that God will reward the doer of evil (referring to himself). It is very obvious that King Saul, with all his pride, arrogance, and envy, would never have made such profound confessions to David if the Almighty God had not made David a god to him (King Saul).

However, David, the servant of God, proved in his character that when a mortal man is being made a god by the Almighty God, he must first of all recognize the will of God in the situation or circumstances wherein he has been made a god, then humble himself in accordance to God's will, in order to effectively execute the noble responsibility of a god.

Also, in like manner, God made Joseph a god to his brothers at the time when they came to Egypt in search of food. During this period, Joseph was second-in-command in Egypt; therefore, he had the power and authority to take revenge against his brothers for attempting to kill him and later selling him into slavery. Joseph instead submitted himself to the will of God, allowing love to rule his heart and take control of his actions – See Genesis 42:1-38, Genesis 43:1-34, Genesis 44:1-34, etc. The above no doubt proves that a "god" with anger, self-will, pride, arrogance, egocentricity, selfishness, vengefulness, malice, and hate cannot, in anyway, walk with the Almighty God to achieve His purpose here on earth.

For instance, it was so sad and unfortunate that the servant of God, Moses, did not make it to the Promised Land, for which he had worked so hard. This was because when the Most High God made him a god to Pharaoh and his people, there was a point in time when he allowed impatience, anger, and self-will to corrupt the "god" spirit within him. This resulted in his disobedience to the Almighty God – Numbers 20:2-13, *"And there was no water for the congregation: and they gathered themselves together against Moses and against Aaron. And the people chode with Moses, and spake, saying, Would God that we had died when our brethren died before the Lord! And why have ye brought up the congregation of the Lord into this wilderness, that we and our cattle should die there? And wherefore have ye made us to come up out of Egypt, to bring us in unto this evil place? it is no place of seed, or of figs, or of vines, or of pomegranates; neither is there any water to drink. And Moses and Aaron went from the presence of the assembly unto the door of the tabernacle of the congregation, and they fell upon their faces: and the glory of the Lord appeared unto them. And the Lord spake unto Moses, saying, Take the rod, and gather thou the assembly together, thou, and Aaron thy brother, and speak ye unto the rock before their eyes; and it shall give forth his water, and thou shalt bring forth to them water out of the rock: so thou shalt give the congregation and their beasts drink. And Moses took the rod from before the Lord, as he commanded him. And Moses and Aaron gathered the congregation together before the rock, and he said unto them, Hear now, ye rebels; must we fetch you water out of this rock? And Moses lifted up his hand, and with his rod he smote the rock twice: and the water came out abundantly, and the congregation drank, and their beasts also. And the Lord spake unto Moses and Aaron, Because ye believed me not, to sanctify me in the eyes of the children of Israel, therefore ye shall not bring this congregation into the land which I have given them. This is the water of Meribah; because the children of Israel strove with the Lord, and he was sanctified in them." Also, Deuteronomy 32:48-52 says, "And the Lord spake unto Moses that selfsame day, saying, Get thee up into this mountain Abarim, unto mount Nebo, which is in the land of Moab, that is over against Jericho; and behold the land of Canaan, which I give unto the children of Israel for a possession: And die in the mount whither thou goest up, and be gathered unto thy people; as Aaron thy brother died in mount Hor, and was gathered unto his people: Because ye trespassed against me among the children of Israel at the waters of MeribahKadesh, in the wilderness of Zin; because ye sanctified me not in the midst of the children of Israel. Yet thou shalt see the land before thee; but thou shalt not go thither unto the land which I give the children of Israel."*

In most cases, impatience can produce anger, then anger in turn produces self-will and arrogance, which ultimately leads to disobedience. This is why humility, patience, and love are the keys to empowering and manifesting the god within us. I wrote in one of my books, "When we allow provocation, bitterness, hate, and resentment to corrupt the good virtues in us, no doubt, we will definitely crash, fail, and live in regret, but when we allow love and patience to lead us, surely, our path will be brightened, and we will be victorious at the end, regardless of what may come our way."

Dearly beloved, it is important that we consistently display the right kind of character in everything that we do and wherever we go, so that the Almighty God will see in us our readiness and willingness to accept the noble responsibility of being a god in our nations, cities, communities, neighborhoods, churches, homes, and even in our very own families. It is obvious that the Most High God wants to make us a god to somebody somewhere, even at this very moment, as I can see through my eyes of faith, but the question of great concern is, "Are we ready and willing to accept this noble, humble, and extraordinary responsibility?" Another question is, "Are we ready and willing to be made a god so that we can take revenge on those who have hurt us or offended us in the past, or do we want to become a god so that we can submit to the will of God and allow ourselves to be graciously used by the Almighty God in achieving His plans and purpose here on earth?"

Beloved of God, how many people have you been a god to in recent times, by demonstrating God's love and kindness or by simply forgiving them of whatever offense or evil that they had done to you in the past? Our God is a Great, Mighty, and Wonderful God, not only because of whom or what He is, but because He shows us compassion and forgives us of our sins unconditionally. However, do we in turn show similar compassion to our fellow human beings and forgive them of the hurt and offenses that they have committed unto us?

When asked by His disciples how many times a man should forgive his offender or those who cause him umbrage, the Lord Jesus Christ told the story of the Kind Creditor and the Wicked Debtor. He related the story to the Kingdom of God and told them that God will deliver those who are unforgiving into eternal torment - Matthew 18:21-35, "*Then came Peter to him, and said, Lord, how oft shall my brother sin against me, and I forgive him? till seven times? Jesus saith unto him, I say not unto thee, Until seven times: but, Until seventy times seven. Therefore is the kingdom of heaven likened unto a certain king, which would take account of his servants. And when he had begun to reckon, one was brought unto him, which owed him ten thousand talents. But forasmuch as he had not to pay, his lord commanded him to be sold, and his wife, and children, and all that he had, and payment to be made. The servant therefore fell down, and worshipped him, saying, Lord, have patience with me, and I will pay thee all. Then the lord of that servant was moved with compassion, and loosed him, and forgave him the debt. But the same servant went out, and found one of his fellowservants, which owed him an hundred pence: and he laid hands on him, and took him by the throat, saying, Pay me that thou owest. And his fellowservant fell down at his feet, and besought him, saying,*

Have patience with me, and I will pay thee all. And he would not: but went and cast him into prison, till he should pay the debt. So when his fellowservants saw what was done, they were very sorry, and came and told unto their lord all that was done. Then his lord, after that he had called him, said unto him, O thou wicked servant, I forgave thee all that debt, because thou desiredst me: Shouldest not thou also have had compassion on thy fellowservant, even as I had pity on thee? And his lord was wroth, and delivered him to the tormentors, till he should pay all that was due unto him. So likewise shall my heavenly Father do also unto you, if ye from your hearts forgive not every one his brother their trespasses."

The above Scripture shows that when we forgive others of their wrong, we no doubt become a god to them. In the above story, the Wicked Debtor displayed an attitude of selfishness, egocentricity, and ungratefulness towards his creditor by refusing to show his fellow servant the same pity and compassion that his master (the Creditor) had shown him. The Debtor's master (the Creditor) became a god to him by borrowing him the money that he needed; thus, meeting him at the point of his needs. In addition to that, he became a god to him by showing him pity and compassion, and forgiving him of his debt when he could not pay back the money that he had borrowed from him. On the contrary, when the Debtor was given a similar opportunity to be a god to his fellow servant, he turned it down, due to his cruelty, selfishness, and egocentricity. Instead of showing pity and compassion to his fellow servant and forgiving his debt as was done to him by his master, he rather assaulted and imprisoned his fellow servant for an amount that was far smaller in value than what he owed his master. This pitiless, cruel, and unsympathetic attitude of the Debtor provoked his master to anger when he heard of the story, so he immediately handed the Wicked Debtor over to the tormentor.

Many people in our world today, including some believers, behave just like the Wicked Debtor. When someone shows them compassion and becomes a god to them by doing good toward them, they often times don't reciprocate that good or even make effort to do similar good to others or show compassion toward them. Instead, they will give an excuse for their selfishness and cruelty and say that it is because they have had bad experiences in the past. They fail to recognize that we are all unique individuals; therefore, we all do not behave the same. When the Most High God shows us kindness and compassion, we must also do the same to others.

Notwithstanding, the story of Jesus Christ and the Ten Lepers teaches us that amongst the hundreds or thousands to whom we will show compassion and help or do good, one will at least return to say, "Glory be to God and thank you, or God bless you." - Luke 17:11-19, *"And it came to pass, as he went to Jerusalem, that he passed through the midst of Samaria and Galilee. And as he entered into a certain village, there met him ten men that were lepers, which stood afar off: And they lifted up their voices, and said, Jesus, Master, have mercy on us. And when he saw them, he said unto them, Go shew yourselves unto the priests. And it came to pass, that, as they went, they were cleansed. And one of them, when he saw that he was healed, turned back, and with a loud voice glorified God, And fell down on his face at his feet, giving him thanks: and he was a Samaritan. And Jesus answering said, Were there not ten cleansed? but where are the nine? There are not found that returned to give glory to God, save this stranger. And he said unto him, Arise, go thy way: thy faith hath made thee whole."*

As children of God, we must realize that our reward is with God and not man; therefore, whatever we do to our fellow man, whether good or bad, it is God who will reward us at the hands of man (someone we may not even know). This is why when you are doing good to a person, do not look at his or her appearance or think of what you can get from that person in return; rather, just let the love of God flow through you and obey the Holy Spirit. This was what the wise man (King Solomon) meant when he urged us to cast our bread upon the water, and we shall receive it after many days. The fact is, water is not a friend of bread, because when water touches bread, it spoils. Likewise, when you cast your bread upon the water, it will spoil, and you are certainly not going to get that bread back. However, this is what we have been told to do, to cast our bread upon the water.

The truth is, when we cast our bread upon the water, it will definitely spoil, and there is no way that we are going to get that identical bread back. The good news is that God Almighty will provide for us a bigger and fresher bread from another source, after we have waited for a while – Ecclesiastes 11:1-2, *"Cast thy bread upon the waters: for thou shalt find it after many days. Give a portion to seven, and also to eight; for thou knowest not what evil shall be upon the earth."* The above simply means that whenever we are doing good to somebody, we are casting our bread upon the water, and we should expect nothing in return from that person. This is also what sowing in tears means, which is why the reward can be so great and unexplainable – Psalm 126:5-6, *"They that sow in tears shall reap in joy. He that goeth forth and weepeth, bearing precious seed, shall doubtless come again with rejoicing, bringing his sheaves with him."*

Henceforth, when we are made gods to our fellow human beings, it is an opportunity and a privilege for us to sow in tears and later reap in joy or cast our bread upon the water and receive it after many days, weeks, months, or years. Being a god is not about our pride, arrogance, or self-will; rather, it is about our humility and total submission to the Holy Spirit of God. Also, being a god is not about seeking our own self-interests; rather, it is about seeking God's interests and allowing God to benefit from us, through our service to Him and to humanity. Based upon this truth of life, I passionately wrote the below poem, **"True Love, Everlasting Love"**:

"True Love, Everlasting Love,
When you think that love is gone
and fearing that life in its fullness is done
Remember that you're not alone
The remedy for healing the wounds of hurt
and despair, is the love that never dies

Oh True Love, Everlasting Love
You're the rock that can never be moved
Your presence is kindness and your touch

is as gentle as a dove that flies as such
You are the Creator of mankind
and the reason for our existence
You are the breath of true lovers
Dashing through the rivers of many waters,
flowing from the humble valley of simplicity,
subduing the great mountains of pride and pomposity

Oh True Love, Everlasting Love,
from whence cometh your power,
and to what extent does your limit goeth?
There is no distance that you cannot reach,
and there is no river or desert you cannot cross
A journey of a million miles, is a journey of one to you
Only those who embrace you will truly acknowledge
that your power is divine and your limit is endless
You are the light that penetrates the darkness of
hate and prejudice, and gravitates all friendships

Oh True Love, Everlasting Love
You are the hope that cements true marriage
The mystery that makes the world go round,
and the wonder that makes imagination a reality
You are the grace that preserves morality and
the force that affine all things
You are the Spirit that transcends man's ego
and the platform on which true greatness stands
You are the foundation on which peace,
tranquility and justice are built

Oh True Love, Everlasting Love
You are the methodical energy that
keeps the flame of our candle ignited
You are the grace that subjects the spirit
of the humble in concinnity with the Great Divine
You are the miracle that transforms
despondency into ecstasy, and war into peace
You are the purest of all virtues,
that is why you are the weapon that engenders
victory into the great battle of life
Whenever you are suppressed or neglected,
evil surfaces, and there's always anger, war, affliction,
cruelty, wickedness, mass death, and destruction
You are the beginning of good and the end of evil
The extinguisher of the fire of segregation
and the resurrection power of integration

Oh True Love, Everlasting Love
You are a foe to the blind and ignorant,
but a friend to the sighted and emancipated
You are the Living God whom we cannot see,
but only perceive your presence
in all that is expressed in nature
You are the perfect timing that concludes
the struggling efforts of mankind
Oh yes, my True Love, my Everlasting Love
when my mortal eyes are humbly closed in death
yes, you will still be there with me in my new birth,

to give me strength for that great Resurrection
O Everlasting Love, you are the mystical spirit
that no man will ever come to comprehend

You are richly blessed and highly favored by the Most High God, Jehovah! Amen!

GRATITUDE

It is indeed a great honor and privilege for me to be given this great opportunity to share the burden of the Almighty God, by graciously and humbly writing this simple book.

All glory, honor, praise, and adoration go to the Most High God of Heaven and Earth, for there is none like Him in the Heaven above, in the earth below, in the sea, and under the earth beneath. Glory and honor also go to my Lord and Savior Jesus Christ of Nazareth for saving my soul and to the Holy Spirit the way He had used me in writing this book.

Franklin D. Todd

www.ingramcontent.com/pod-product-compliance
Lightning Source LLC
Chambersburg PA
CBHW020241010526
44107CB00039B/1462/J